God's Covenant
For Your Family

God's Covenant
For Your Family

by
Marilyn Hickey

Marilyn
Hickey
Ministries

P.O. Box 17340
Denver, Colorado 80217

God's Covenant For Your Family
ISBN 0-89274-245-3
Copyright © 1982 by Marilyn Hickey
Laymen's Library

Contents

God's Covenant
For Your Family

1

God's Covenant For Your Family

God has lots of good things for you and your family. They are all part of His covenant with you as His child. We usually think of a covenant in a negative sense, as something that we must do or else suffer a penalty. But basically God's covenant is positive. It involves receiving those things that God has promised to us. When you entered into God's new covenant, many promises became yours — promises not only for you, but also for your mate and for your children.

I want to look with you at the covenant relationship of marriage — the original covenant — the unfolding of this covenant, and what it means to you, to your mate, and to your children.

The Husband and Wife Covenant

We usually think of a covenant as only a relationship with God, but the Bible says there is a covenant in marriage:

> Yet ye say, Wherefore? Because the Lord hath been witness between thee and the wife of thy youth, against whom thou

9

hast dealt treacherously: yet is she thy companion, and the wife of thy covenant.
                                    Malachi 2:14

This scripture reveals that there is a covenant relationship in marriage. Married Christians have a covenant relationship with the Father, and with each other. When you belong to God and enter into a marriage contract, that marriage is a covenant between you and your mate. If you were not born again when you married, then you did not enter into the covenant described here in Malachi. But if you and your mate were born again when you wed, then in God's eyes your relationship is a covenant.

There is another scripture that shows the existence of a covenant relationship in marriage:

To deliver thee from the strange woman, even from the stranger which flattereth with her words; which forsaketh the guide of her youth, and forgetteth the covenant of her God.
                                    Proverbs 2:16,17

The *covenant of her God* mentioned here refers to marriage. This woman entered into a covenant with her husband as a young person, but now she has forgotten it. She has tossed aside her marriage relationship. She does not count it as important; nevertheless, it is a covenant relationship.

Early Covenants

The word *covenant* always means "to cut." In olden times when people "cut a covenant," they would cut their wrists and let the blood drip into a cup. They would then each drink out of that common cup. By so doing, they were saying, "Now we are one."

One of the first illustrations of a covenant is found in the story of Cain and Abel. (Gen. 4:1-8.) Abel offered an animal as a sacrifice to God, while Cain offered Him the fruit of the ground. God accepted Abel's sacrifice, but rejected Cain's. Why?

Because Abel was in essence saying, "I want to enter into a covenant relationship with You. I want to intermingle and be one with You." He cut a covenant with God. There was the shedding of blood. Cain, on the other hand, made no attempt at a covenant relationship. You can't bring God a bunch of grapes as a covenant because there is no blood in them: . . . *without shedding of blood there is no forgiveness* (Heb. 9:22 NASB).

Proverbs 18:24 speaks of *a friend that sticketh closer than a brother*. That is a covenant friend. You may have a natural, blood brother, but a friend with whom you have cut a covenant is closer to you. You have intermingled your blood with his and have become one by an act of your will. You have exchanged your lives. You have intermingled your natures.

11

Family Covenant

The covenant relationship expands to take in an entire family when God deals with Noah. Noah built the ark according to the instructions of God, and after he built it, his family entered it.

God didn't say, "Come on into the ark, Noah." He said, *Come thou and all thy household into the ark* (Gen. 7:1). God wanted all of Noah's family saved. Noah and his household went into the ark and were safe during the terrible storm. At the end of the storm, Noah came out and offered a sacrifice of animals. He cut a covenant with God.

God, in return, said that He would make a covenant with Noah. He said, "I'm going to put a rainbow in the sky, and I will never again totally cover the earth with water." (Gen. 9:11-16.) That covenant benefited Noah's whole family.

Abraham is another man who enjoyed a covenant relationship with God. The Bible refers to Abraham as being the friend of God:

> *And the scripture was fulfilled which saith, Abraham believed God, and it was imputed unto him for righteousness: and he was called the Friend of God.*
>
> *James 2:23*

> *But thou, Israel, art my servant, Jacob whom I have chosen, the seed of Abraham my friend.*
>
> *Isaiah 41:8*

> *Art not thou our God, who didst drive*
> *out the inhabitants of this land before thy*
> *people Israel, and gavest it to the seed of*
> *Abraham thy friend for ever?*
>   *2 Chronicles 20:7,8*

God gave the Promised Land to the seed of Abraham, His friend. The word for *friend* here does not mean "neighbor." There are two Hebrew words used in the Old Testament for *friend*. When the word *neighbor* is used in Proverbs, for instance, it usually means just an acquaintance, someone you live next to; a casual, surface friendship. But the word for *friend* used here means "a loving one." Friends are very, very close to each other. Friendship is a covenant relationship.

The Bible also tells us that *Abraham believed God, and it was imputed unto him for righteousness* (James 2:23). When it says that Abraham "believed God," it doesn't mean the casual "I believe in God" attitude. (The devils believe in God!) It means, rather, an unqualified committal. Abraham was saying, "God, I give myself to You without any strings attached." And in return God said, "Abraham, I give Myself to you totally, without any reservation."

God's covenant with Abraham was different from those which preceded it. This covenant was not based on just a sacrifice of an animal. God said, "Abraham, I'm going to make a covenant with you,

13

and I want you to be circumcised." (Gen. 17:10.) Circumcision involves the cutting of the human body and the shedding of human blood.

Why did God require that of Abraham? Why couldn't an animal have been substituted? Because God was saying to Abraham, "My covenant is not only with you, it is with all the seed that will come forth from you. I have a covenant with them also. When I say that I'm going to do good things for you, that includes every seed that comes from you. I have a covenant with you and your seed." (Gen. 17:7.)

Under the old Hebrew law, custom, and tradition, every newborn Jewish boy was circumcised on the eighth day. Present at that circumcision rite was the boy's godfather. When that little boy was circumcised, he entered into the same covenant relationship with God that Abraham had; and all his seed entered into that same covenant. The godfather was there to see that the child lived out that covenant.

Abraham's covenant with God was a covenant of friendship. They loved each other; they were like one. God said, "I give Myself totally to you, Abraham, and you give yourself totally to me, you and all your seed. That's why I had you circumcised. I wanted that to be a sign forever that all your seed would enter into the covenant too. Abraham, I want your household to be a part of the covenant relationship with Me."

It wasn't long, however, before the covenant relationship was tested. God said to Abraham, "Do you truly give yourself to Me without qualification? You've got a seed, and you waited a long time to get him. Now I want you to give him back to Me. Abraham, are we covenant friends? Did you really enter that covenant and say that you gave yourself to me without reserve? If you did, it means that you will give up your son for Me." (Gen. 22:1-3.)

So Abraham went upon a mountain to do as God had commanded. By his obedience Abraham was saying to God, "I will sacrifice my son to You. I'll do it because I believe that You can even raise him from the ashes. You promised that my seed would be as the dust of the earth and the sand of the sea, even as the stars of the heavens. You will raise Isaac from the dead. I trust You because You've already given me Your Word. I trust You. I'm Your friend." (vv. 3-10.)

A friend sticks closer than a brother. True friendship is a covenant relationship. It is two friends who have entered into the intermingling of natures. As you probably know, Abraham didn't have to sacrifice Isaac; God provided His own lamb for the sacrifice. By His actions God was saying to Abraham, "I'm your friend, and I'm the friend of all your seed." (vv. 11-13.)

New Testament Covenant Friends

Jesus spoke of friends in the New Testament:

*Greater love hath no man than this,
that a man lay down his life for his friends.*

*Ye are my friends, if ye do whatsoever
I command you.*

John 14:13,14

What kind of friends? Casual acquaintances?
No. Covenant friends, because covenant friends will
die for each other. They will do anything for each
other. They are willing to shed their blood for each
other. Jesus says, "You are My friends, if you do
whatever I command you. You are My covenant
friends if you do My Word."

Who are His covenant friends? You and I. We
are God's friends. Jesus laid down His life for us.
There was the shedding of blood for this covenant.
We have entered into His covenant relationship. We
are the seed of Abraham. All of the covenant
promises — all the things that God promised
Abraham — belong to us because we are God's
friends.

We have become a part of the new covenant
because we accepted the shedding of Jesus' blood for
our sins.

*Then Jesus said unto them, Verily,
verily, I say unto you, Except ye eat the
flesh of the Son of man, and drink his blood,
ye have no life in you.*

16

*Whoso eateth my flesh, and drinketh
my blood, hath eternal life; and I will raise
him up at the last day.*

*For my flesh is meat indeed, and my
blood is drink indeed.*

*He that eateth my flesh, and drinketh
my blood, dwelleth in me, and I in him.*
                                    John 6:53-56

In effect, Jesus was saying, "I want to enter into
a covenant relationship with you. If you drink My
blood [as when the wrists were cut and the blood
intermingled and drunk from the cup], then our
natures will intermingle. If you eat of My flesh [a
covenant relationship was always celebrated with a
feast], then you're Mine."

Now we can't literally drink Christ's blood, but
when we accepted Jesus, we by faith partook of His
blood. We sing about His blood flowing through us
and through our veins, and we sing about our being a
part of the King. Why? Because we have entered into
a covenant relationship with Christ, and we have the
nature of Jesus flowing through us.

We have given ourselves unqualifiedly to Him.
We have cut the covenant with Him by eating His
flesh and drinking His blood. His flesh is meat or
bread:

*This is that bread which came down
from heaven: not as your fathers did eat*

manna, and are dead: he that eateth of this
bread shall live for ever.

John 6:58

How do you eat this bread?

It is the spirit that quickeneth; the
flesh profiteth nothing: the words that I
speak unto you, they are spirit, and they
are life.

John 6:63

When you eat the Word of Christ, you are eating His flesh. We have entered into a covenant relationship. We belong to Jesus and He belongs to us without qualification. He is our friend. God gave up the life of His only Son for all of Abraham's seed. He cut the covenant with us by the shedding of blood, and we have entered into that relationship.

Abraham was called the friend of God, and now we are friends of God. When we entered into the new covenant, we found a Friend that sticks closer than a brother. It is not enough for us to have blood relationships within our families. We need to have a covenant relationship with Jesus Christ which includes all of our family members.

There is an unusual passage in Exodus which helps explain the importance of the covenant relationship:

And Moses took his wife (Zipporah)
and his sons, and set them upon an ass, and
he returned to the land of Egypt . . .

And it came to pass by the way in the inn, that the Lord met him (Moses' son) and sought to kill him.

Then Zipporah took a sharp stone, and cut off the foreskin of her son, and cast it at his feet, and said, Surely a bloody husband art thou to me.

So he let him go: then she said, A bloody husband thou art, because of the circumcision.

Exodus 4:20,24-26

Who was about to get killed? Moses' son. Why? Because he had not yet been circumcised. He had not entered into the covenant. God was saying to Moses, "You're going down to Egypt unprepared. You've got to have your family in the covenant also, or else they can be harmed or killed." That's how strong the covenant relationship is. God wants your children in the covenant relationship so they can be protected.

Moses and his family were going into enemy territory where there were magicians and all kinds of strange things. God was telling Moses that his children had to be in on the covenant or they would be in danger. He was saying, "I'd rather take their lives now than let them go down to Egypt and be taken by some magician."

Evidently Zipporah had objected up to this time to her son's being circumcised, but now she says,

"Circumcise him! You are a bloody husband to me."
She knew that Moses was a man of the blood
covenant.

The Blood Covenant

In the twelfth chapter of Exodus the Bible tells
us that God spoke to Moses and said, "I want you to
take a lamb and shed the blood of it. Kill it at the
doorway, right in the door of the house. There is to be
a lamb for each house. Take the blood and put it over
the door posts and on each side of the entrance.
When the death angel passes over, the firstborn on
the inside of that house will not be killed. There will
be safety within that house." (Ex. 12:3-13.)

Here God is again cutting the covenant. This
covenant is not just for one person, but for the entire
household.

Then God said to the children of Israel, "It is
through the shedding of blood that we have a
covenant, and I want you to do something that will
always remind you of this covenant between us:

> And it shall be when the Lord shall
> bring thee into the land of the Canaanites,
> as he sware unto thee and to thy fathers,
> and shall give it thee, that thou shalt set
> apart unto the Lord all that openeth the
> matrix, and every firstling that cometh of a
> beast which thou hast; the males shall be
> the Lord's . . .

And it shall be when thy son asketh thee in time to come, saying, What is this? that thou shalt say unto him, By strength of hand the Lord brought us out from Egypt, from the house of bondage:

And it came to pass, when Pharaoh would hardly let us go, that the Lord slew all the firstborn in the land of Egypt, both the firstborn of man, and the firstborn of beast: therefore I sacrifice to the Lord all that openeth the matrix, being males; but all the firstborn of my children I redeem.

And it shall be for a token upon thine hand, and for frontlets between thine eyes: for by strength of hand the Lord brought us forth out of Egypt.

Exodus 13:11-16

These people had to wear a phylactery (a small leather case) on their foreheads. Inside this phylactery were all the scriptures of redemption through the shedding of blood for their families. On their wrists they had to wear a little bracelet which also contained a roll of scriptures with the plan of redemption through the shedding of blood.

Now, there was the shedding of blood to enter into the covenant, and there also was the wearing of the Word that said what the covenant meant. In the New Testament we find the parallel to this in

Revelation 12:11: *They* (the brethren) *overcame him* (Satan) *by the blood of the Lamb, and by the word of their testimony.* We believers overcome the Devil by the blood of the Lamb, **and** by the Word of our testimony. Jesus said that whoever drinks of His blood and eats of His flesh (the Word) is part of the covenant. We must partake of Jesus' shed blood, but we must also partake of the Word. Circumcision was never enough; it had to be combined with the Word.

> *And these words, which I command thee this day, shall be in thine heart: and thou shalt teach them diligently unto thy children, and shalt talk of them when thou sittest in thine house, and when thou walkest by the way, and when thou liest down, and when thou risest up.*
>
> *And thou shalt bind them for a sign upon thine hand, and they shall be as frontlets between thine eyes.*
>
> *And thou shalt write them upon the posts of thy house, and on thy gates.*
>
> Deuteronomy 6:6-9

It isn't enough just to have your children born again. You must give them the Word every place you go. When we become involved in the covenant, we are also to bring in our whole household. They are not just to be born again; they are to be saturated with the Word. The blood and the Word cannot be separated. Our covenant relationship with God is based upon both.

The Marriage Covenant

When we Christians wed, we enter into a marriage covenant. We not only have a covenant with the Father, we also have a covenant with our mates. In the beginning God said, "I will make Adam and Eve as one flesh." He even took the bone out of Adam to make Eve. He said, "I will make them one. They will cling to each other; they will have a covenant relationship because they will be as one." (Gen. 2:24.)

Jesus said, . . . *What therefore God hath joined together, let not man put asunder* (Matt. 19:6). Why? Because marriage partners are in covenant relationship. They are like one, and have the intermingling of natures. They have a covenant with God and with each other. Because of that, all of the children who come from that marriage belong to God and enter into the covenant promises.

Paul illustrates this covenant relationship in Ephesians when he says, *Husbands, love your wives, even as Christ also loved the church, and gave himself for it* (Eph. 5:25). How is a husband to love his wife? He is to love her as Christ loves the Church. Paul commands him to do this. Someone might say, "If you had my wife, you wouldn't love her. She is terrible. She doesn't keep house, she looks ugly, she smells, she doesn't cook, she's mean to the children, and she's nasty to me." But the Bible doesn't say, "Husbands, love your wives because she does all the right things." It just says, "Husbands, love your wives because you are in covenant relationship."

A good example of this relationship is found in the Old Testament. Jacob had two wives, Leah and Rachel. He never wanted Leah; he got stuck with her. He worked seven years to get Rachel, but got Leah instead. He had to work seven more years for Rachel. Fourteen years he worked to get Rachel, and he still had to keep Leah!

Leah was ugly, and Jacob didn't love her. But God wanted Jacob to love his wife; so to help him love Leah, He closed up Rachel's womb and only gave Jacob children through Leah. Why? Because we are not supposed to love by emotion. We are supposed to love by faith. That's why some people fall out of love with their mates; they try to love by emotion and sight rather than by faith.

Eventually Jacob learned the lesson. Since God later opened Rachel's womb and gave her a child, Jacob must have finally learned to love Leah. It may not have been easy at first. He probably went to her and said, not too enthusiastically, "Leah, I love you." It was likely said less than wholeheartedly, but it was a start. And that's faith, isn't it? Jacob certainly wasn't walking by sight. But each time he said, "Leah, I love you," it became a little easier.

But that isn't the end of the story. When Jacob was buried, he wasn't buried with Rachel. Before he died, he asked to be buried with Leah. When he began saying, "Leah, I love you," he started to feel it. He walked by faith, and it changed his life and his feelings about Leah. If your marriage is not working as you live by sight, try living it by faith!

Paul shows what the covenant relationship means between Christ and His Church and between a husband and his wife:

> *Husbands, love your wives, even as Christ also loved the church, and gave himself for it; that he might sanctify and cleanse it with the washing of water by the word . . .*
>
> *For we are members of his body, of his flesh, and of his bones.*
>
> *Ephesians 5:25,26,30*

Christ and the Church are one. A husband and wife are one. The Church is *of his flesh, and of his bones.* When Adam saw Eve, that's what he said, "She's bone of my bone and flesh of my flesh." (Gen. 2:23.) There is a covenant relationship that makes Christ and the Church one, and there is a covenant relationship that makes a husband and wife one.

Jonathan and David are another example of two people who entered into a covenant relationship. (1 Sam. 18:3,4.) When they entered into covenant, they exchanged coats. They exchanged weapons. They vowed to each other, "If anything happens to you, I'll take care of your children." There is no question that David took care of Mephibosheth, Jonathan's son, after Jonathan's death. (2 Sam. 9:1-13.)

When we entered into a covenant relationship with God, we exchanged clothing. What did we give God? Our dirty rags of unrighteousness. What did He give us? A robe of righteousness. The Bible says we are the righteousness of God in Christ Jesus. (2 Cor. 5:21.) Aren't you glad you swapped!

What else did we exchange? Our weakness for His strength. He gave us His weapon — the Word. The Word is our sword.

The Family Covenant

Because you are in covenant relationship with God and with your mate, you have the right to claim God's promises for your seed.

> *And all thy children shall be taught of the Lord; and great shall be the peace of thy children.*
>
> Isaiah 54:13

> *I call heaven and earth to record this day against you, that I have set before you life and death, blessing and cursing:*

therefore choose life, that both thou and thy seed may live.

> *Deuteronomy 30:19*

Praise ye the Lord. Blessed is the man that feareth the Lord, that delighteth greatly in his commandments.

His seed shall be mighty upon the earth: the generation of the upright shall be blessed.

Wealth and riches shall be in his house: and his righteousness endureth for ever . . .

He hath dispersed, he hath given to the poor; his righteousness endureth for ever; his horn shall be exalted with honour.

> *Psalm 112:1-3,9*

God is concerned about the peace of your children. He wants to bless you and your family, but you must choose the blessing. You must choose life for yourself and for your children. And life comes through God's Word.

Did you know that your children are supposed to be mighty? It's not enough to see them just make it into heaven. They are to be mighty! They are part of the covenant relationship. Don't settle for anything less! There is supposed to be wealth and riches in your house and in the house of your seed. They aren't supposed to be poor anymore than you are.

How do you build your house?

*Through wisdom is an house builded;
and by understanding it is established: and
by knowledge shall the chambers be filled
with all precious and pleasant riches . . .*

*Lay not wait, O wicked man, against
the dwelling of the righteous; spoil not his
resting place.*

Proverbs 24:3,4,15

Give your seed the Word. Pray and confess the
Word with them. Get them to confess the Word that
they can do all things through Christ Who
strengthens them. (Phil. 4:13.)

Get the Word into your children when they are
young. One time my son Mike bought a jump rope. I
had never tried to jump rope, and he said to me,
"Mother, you need it. It will help you. You need to
exercise."

"All right," I said, "if you'll teach me how."

We went out on the back porch, and I was really
having a hard time. I said, "Oh, Mike, I've never
been able to jump rope. I just can't do it."

"Mother," he said, "you can do all things
through Christ Who strengthens you!"

Thank you, Mike. I needed that! He'd heard that
enough from me, and it was good for him to give it
back to me.

If you are not giving the Word to your children, you are not building your house in wisdom and instruction. Fill your house with the Word, and the house will fill up with riches and wealth. And notice one other thing: the wicked can't touch the house of the righteous because the Word is there. (Prov. 24:15.) Our families are in covenant relationship with God, and we overcome the Devil by the blood of the Lamb and by the Word of our testimony. The blood and the Word put our family over! It worked in Moses' day, and it works in our day.

The Bible has more to say about your household:

> *The house of the wicked shall be overthrown: but the tabernacle of the upright shall flourish.*
>
> *Proverbs 14:11*

Remember Cornelius in the book of Acts? He sowed alms and prayed; he was a devout man. When Peter was sent there to preach, Cornelius and his household received the Holy Spirit. (Acts 10:1-48.) Expect the same for your household.

> *For the promise is unto you, and to your children, and to all that are afar off, even as many as the Lord our God shall call.*
>
> *Acts 2:39*

Don't ever be satisfied until your children are Spirit-filled. My daughter Sarah was Spirit-filled when she was four years old. We were cleaning house together one day, and I was talking to her about the baptism in the Holy Spirit. She said, "Mother, I'm going to be baptized in the Holy Spirit."

"Honey, I know you will be." I was thinking that it would happen when she was seven, eight, or even nine years old.

She said, "I'm going to be baptized in the Holy Spirit today."

I thought, *That's sweet.* But I really didn't believe it.

She said, "After I get up from my nap I will be Spirit-filled."

"How will you know it?" I asked.

"Because I will be speaking in tongues," she said confidently.

I put her to bed for her nap, and she slept for about two hours. When I went in to get her up, she was sitting up in the bed speaking in tongues and smiling. I had been claiming Acts 2:39 for my seed, but I didn't expect it at four years of age! But God's promise is good for any age. His promise is unto my children. Claim His promise for your children as well!

The account of the Philippian jailer in the sixteenth chapter of Acts shows that God is concerned with households. The jailer beat Paul and

Silas and did nothing to treat their wounds. He put them in the worst part of the jail, stuck their feet in the stocks, went home, and forgot about them.

Paul and Silas began to sing, and the prisoners listened. The verb for *listened* in this passage means "to listen with pleasure." The prisoners were listening to the praises being given, and it was bringing pleasure to them. God sent an earthquake which woke the jailer. The music didn't wake him, but the earthquake did!

The jailer knew that if any of the prisoners escaped, it would mean his life. That was Roman law. He was ready to kill himself, but Paul shouted to him, "Don't do it! We are all here." The jailer was so shocked that he brought Paul and Silas out and asked them, *Sirs, what must I do to be saved?* (Acts 16:30).

The evening before, he had beat them. Now he addresses them as "Sirs." Paul answered him by saying, *Believe on the Lord Jesus Christ, and thou shalt be saved, and thy house* (v. 31).

Why did Paul say *house*? Because salvation is a covenant relationship, and Paul knew that it was for the household too. The jailer took them to his home, washed their wounds, and set a table before them. The Twenty-Third Psalm says that God sets a table before us in the presence of our enemies. (v. 5.) That Philippian jailer was an enemy who became Paul's covenant friend. Not only did the jailer get saved, his whole household entered into covenant relationship.

One other point about this family covenant which needs to be mentioned concerns Paul's statement in 1 Corinthians 7:14: *For the unbelieving husband is sanctified by the wife, and the unbelieving wife is sanctified by the husband.* When we are born again, we enter into a covenant relationship. This includes our mates, no matter how mean and nasty they may be. Even if they are not yet saved, there is still a portion of the covenant relationship that covers them. One believing mate sanctifies a household, and he or she can believe for the other unsaved members. Don't give up because your mate is unsaved or because the circumstances seem bad.

If things look bad, remember Hannah. She placed her son Samuel in the care of Eli, who was in a backslidden condition along with his sons. His sons were so corrupt they even committed adultery right in the temple in front of Samuel! Did it affect Samuel? No, because his mother had sown the Word, and the Word was more powerful than circumstances, environment, or heredity. The believing mate will sanctify the household because of the covenant relationship. But for you to be able to do this, you must have the blood and the Word — it takes both.

Lastly, don't ever be defeated by the old lie that says, "But other people have a will of their own." Certainly they have a will, but John 17:2 says that

Jesus has power over **all** flesh, and that includes the will. The Word is bigger than the will. Look in the mirror and remember that the Word changed **your** will!

Pray this prayer and thank the Lord for the covenant position into which you have been brought. Thank Him for His promises concerning your mate and your children:

Father, I thank You today that I have accepted the shedding of Your Son's blood and have entered into covenant relationship with You. Thank You that we are friends.

I thank You that I have the Word for myself and for my family. My household is sanctified by my covenant relationship with You. I claim all the promises for my children that are found in Your Word, and I praise You for the power in the blood and in the Word to bring all this to pass. Amen.

2

Sex — For Married People Only

God made man and woman as threefold beings: spirit, soul, and body. He is concerned about our total existence — spiritual, emotional, and physical. All three areas of our lives should be fulfilling and delightful.

Dick Mills once said, "I believe it will only be the Christians who will have a happy, delightful, normal physical relationship in the latter days." I think this statement is correct because we see all kinds of perverted sex today — homosexuality, lesbianism, and everything imaginable (and unimaginable!). Sex without love, apart from God's guidelines, is unhappy and unfulfilling.

The Bible has much to say about the physical relationship in marriage, and much of what it says may surprise many people. God is concerned that we have a very delightful relationship. Sex is not something to be embarrassed about, and it is not something "just for having children." A right understanding of this area in a marriage is vital to achieve a happy, healthy family and home.

Adam's Helpmeet

> *And the Lord God said, It is not good that man should be alone; I will make him an help meet for him.*
>
> Genesis 2:18

There has been much misunderstanding regarding a wife's relationship to her husband. Eve was to be a "help meet" for Adam. A "help meet" is an alter ego, someone who complements the husband. To *complement* means "to complete or bring to perfection, something added to complete a whole." A husband and wife make a complete picture of a home.

Rather than be a slave or a servant, the woman was added to the man for the purpose of completion. Sometimes when I talk to wives, they will say, "My husband takes total care of bringing home the check, but I pay all the bills. I'm the bookkeeper for the household. He can't keep a checkbook at all."

Then someone else (like me!) will say, "If I kept the checkbook, who knows what would happen! My husband writes all our checks and pays all the bills." Is this practice wrong, or is it right? Neither. One time my husband really got after me about my checkbook, and I said, "Well, don't you understand why the Lord had me marry you? It's because He saw that I was lacking in this area, and He gave me to you so that you could help me!"

Marriage partners are to complement each other, not compete with each other. If there is an area where you are lacking and your spouse is a help, that's wonderful. Together you make a complete, beautiful picture. When your relationship is complete, you complement each other. You are one, and Jesus makes the two of you complete, for we are complete in Him.

God said, "I see that Adam needs an helpmeet, someone to meet his needs, and someone whose needs he can meet." The Bible tells us that God made all of His creation to be "very good." (Gen. 1:31.) He made the man and woman to be very good, and their relationship should be very good also.

When Adam saw Eve for the first time, he said, *This is now bone of my bones, and flesh of my flesh: she shall be called Woman, because she was taken out of Man* (Gen. 2:23).

They were to be one flesh. The Bible says that they were to go out and multiply in the earth, which necessitates physical union. God said that first. (Gen. 1:28.) And He said that it was very good. He wasn't stuffy about it in any way. The "one flesh" relationship was ordained by God, and it was to be very good.

We're not just talking "Old Testament" here. Jesus also referred to this union in the New Testament. The New Testament is built upon the Old

37

Testament, and together they represent a complete picture.

> *The Pharisees also came unto him, tempting him, and saying unto him, Is it lawful for a man to put away his wife for every cause?*
>
> *And he answered and said unto them, Have ye not read, that he which made them at the beginning made them male and female, and said, For this cause shall a man leave father and mother, and shall cleave to his wife: and they twain shall be one flesh?*
>
> Matthew 19:3-5

Jesus talked of a man's "cleaving" unto his wife. That has to do with a physical relationship. Jesus didn't mention children first; He mentioned the physical relationship first. It is mentioned that way in the Old Testament, and Jesus refers to it in the New Testament in that order.

The entire Bible has much to say about the marriage relationship. The twenty-fourth chapter of Genesis talks about the relationship of Isaac and Rebekah. Abraham's servant Eliezer was sent to find a wife for Abraham's son, Isaac. God led him to Rebekah and he brought her back to Isaac. She was God's choice for him.

> Isaac brought her into his mother
> Sarah's tent, and took Rebekah, and she
> became his wife; and he loved her: and
> Isaac was comforted after his mother's
> death.
>
> > *Genesis 24:67*

The physical relationship should bring comfort and strength. (The word translated "comfort" here also means "strength.") These two qualities belong to a marital relationship.

Solomon's Wisdom

Solomon has a great deal to say about the physical relationship. He is very honest and helpful in this respect. He sets forth the guidelines and the boundaries of the physical relationship.

> *Live joyfully with the wife whom thou
> lovest all the days of the life of thy vanity,
> which he (God) hath given thee under the
> sun.*
>
> > *Ecclesiastes 9:9*

Live joyfully with her! Marriage should be a delightful relationship, not a drag. It should be great!

Solomon paints a beautiful picture of the marital relationship in Proverbs 5:15-19:

> *Drink waters out of thine own cistern,
> and running waters out of thine own well.*

Let thy fountains be dispersed abroad, and rivers of waters in the streets.

Let them be only thine own, and not strangers' with thee.

Let thy fountain be blessed: and rejoice with the wife of thy youth.

Let her be as the loving hind and pleasant roe; let her breasts satisfy thee at all times; and be thou ravished always with her love.

Straightforward, isn't he! A marital relationship should be tremendous! Each partner should be wild over the other. I can hear someone saying, "I don't think my marriage is like that." Then start claiming these scriptures so that it will be!

Recently, I had a counseling session with a young girl who had only been married a couple of months. She told me that her physical relationship with her husband was practically nothing. "Should it be like that?" she asked. "We are just newly married." No, it should not be like that!

We talked for a while and then God quickened scripture passages to me. One of them was Proverbs 5:15-19. I told her that she should begin to claim this promised fulfillment in her marriage relationship. "Begin to claim that your relationship is great," I told her, "that it is absolutely delightful!"

I like what Proverbs 5 says, ". . . waters . . . fountain . . . ." In other words, the physical relationship in marriage is to be refreshing, as refreshing as a good drink of cold water when you are really thirsty. You don't give up drinking water when you reach the age of thirty-five, do you? No, you drink water until you die.

Oh, come on, Marilyn. You don't believe that physical love can last a lifetime, do you?

Yes! I do! The Bible says that Moses' natural force was not abated, nor his eye dim when he was one hundred and twenty years old. (Deut. 34:7.) People don't have to lose their sex life as they grow older. We're to . . . *live joyfully . . . all the days* of our lives.

The physical relationship is to be a fountain that flows all the time, and it is to be a wonderful thing. I notice something else about this cistern. At the beginning of Proverbs 5, Solomon speaks of a physical relationship as being wisdom:

> *My son, attend unto my wisdom, and*
> *bow thine ear to my understanding.*
> *Proverbs 5:1*

To have a good, strong physical relationship — one that is refreshing, one that is continuing — is wisdom!

For the ways of man are before the eyes of the Lord, and he pondereth all his goings.

Proverbs 5:21

God is watching your physical relationship with your mate. He is concerned about it because He knows it is important.

Paul's Wisdom

The Apostle Paul lays down some very strong guidelines for the marital relationship. His instruction points up the importance that God places on this area of marriage:

Now concerning the things whereof ye wrote unto me: It is good for a man not to touch a woman.

Nevertheless, to avoid fornication, let every man have his own wife, and let every woman have her own husband.

Let the husband render unto the wife due benevolence: and likewise also the wife unto the husband.

The wife hath not power of her own body, but the husband: and likewise also the husband hath not power of his own body, but the wife.

Defraud ye not one the other, except it be with consent for a time, that ye may give yourselves to fasting and prayer; and come together again, that Satan tempt you not for your incontinency.

1 *Corinthians* 7:1-5

What is this "due benevolence" which the husband is to render to his wife? It doesn't mean just being polite to her. Paul is saying here that it is just as important for the woman to be satisfied in the physical realm as it is for the man. Did you ever hear anything like this when you were growing up: "A woman is never satisfied in lovemaking, and she shouldn't expect to be. That's just the way it is." "Due benevolence" means that the woman should be just as delighted in physical love as her husband. Some women think this is not scriptural, but it is!

Paul says, *Defraud ye not one another.* In other words, don't put one another off, except by mutual consent, in order to give yourselves to fasting and prayer. Then . . . *come together again, that Satan tempt you not for your incontinency.* Did you ever notice that Paul equates the physical life with the prayer life? Some people like to act "spiritual" and talk of "fasting and prayer." Yes, you're supposed to fast and pray, but Paul also says that you are to have a physical relationship too! Paul puts the two on an equal basis. That's how important physical love is.

Sometimes when a woman (especially) gets saved and Spirit-filled, and her husband is not, she becomes too "spiritual" to have any physical relationship. She cuts her husband off, and then wonders why he never gets saved. It is not what the Bible says to do!

The Bible says that marriage partners are not to put each other off unless it is with mutual consent. "Defrauding" one another means not allowing the other person to be satisfied. I think this area is more of a problem in marriage than anything else, as far as the physical relationship is concerned. Each mate should be concerned that the other is fully and totally satisfied. Both partners have a responsibility to meet the other's needs.

Hebrews 13:4 says, *Marriage is honourable in all, and the bed undefiled: but whoremongers and adulterers God will judge.* Every aspect of marriage is honorable, which includes the physical relationship. But a physical relationship outside marriage will be judged by God. What does *undefiled* mean? It means "unsoiled and pure." It means that there should be no abnormal sexual act. There is not to be anything in the realm of homosexuality or lesbianism. There is to be a pure love relationship between the husband and wife.

The Bible tells us from the very beginning about a woman and her physical relationship:

> *Unto the woman he (God) said, I will greatly multiply thy sorrow and thy conception; in sorrow thou shalt bring*

44

> *forth children; and thy desire shall be to*
> *thy husband, and he shall rule over thee.*
>
> Genesis 3:16

Although God told the woman, "I will greatly multiply your sorrow and conception," I do not believe that we women are under the curse any longer, because in Jesus Christ we are all new creatures.

We should not overlook the little nugget of truth found in the words, . . . *thy desire shall be to thy husband.* What does *desire* mean? It means "stretching forth or longing." A woman should have a longing for her husband. There is nothing wrong with that; and, in fact, there is something wrong if a wife doesn't have a desire for her husband.

I believe that Sarah, Abraham's wife, was a woman who enjoyed her physical relationship with her husband. Look closely at Genesis 18:12:

> *Therefore Sarah laughed within*
> *herself, saying, After I am waxed old shall I*
> *have pleasure, my lord being old also?*

Sarah eavesdropped and heard God tell Abraham that she was supposed to have a baby within a year. She ". . . laughed within herself" at the thought of her and Abraham's having a child. It doesn't sound to me like Sarah's physical relationship was a drag; her laughter makes it sound like it was terrific!

The marriage relationship should just keep getting better and better. When you are one with your mate — spiritually and physically, mentally and emotionally — your marriage goes from good to better to best! King Solomon had much to say about this in the Song of Solomon, chapters 6, 7, and 8. He was ravished with his beloved and fully satisfied with his relationship. You can be too!

Solomon's Warning

The Bible has many wonderful things to say about the physical relationship in a marriage. It also gives many warnings to the person who seeks to fulfill a physical desire outside the marriage relationship. God's restrictions in this area are not given to restrict our happiness, but to restrict our **un**happiness. The results of sex outside marriage are tragic. A man or woman involved in a physical relationship outside marriage can prevent children from being born of that relationship, but they cannot prevent the damage that is inflicted upon the soul and the conscience.

In the fifth chapter of Proverbs Solomon gives his son wisdom in the area of unfaithfulness. I think that some (not all) unfaithfulness is a result of one partner failing to satisfy the other. When a person falls into adultery because he or she has been refused or defrauded by their mate, I believe that mate shares some of the responsibility for that adulterous action in the sight of God.

We have some friends who used to live in Denver. One time the husband told us, "My wife just kind of takes our marriage for granted. When I married her, she was attractive. She always dressed up and looked nice. We have three children now, and when I come home at night and she meets me at the door, she either has curlers in her hair or leaves it hanging down straight. She flops around in an old housecoat. A lot of times she smells bad. She acts indifferent to me. I work in an office with beautiful secretaries. They keep themselves well groomed. Their hair looks nice and they smell good. I can't help but smell them and see them, and it is very tempting to me. Meanwhile my wife acts very uninterested in our physical life."

I told that man's wife what her husband had said. She said, "I don't want that happening to my marriage!" She had unknowingly become uninterested in their relationship. Her attitude and actions could have pushed her husband into an adulterous affair.

That's why I say that the physical relationship is a very important part of any marriage. It's an area that needs to be strengthened and continued as you grow older. Constantly look for ways to improve your appearance. Husband **and** wife should always be attractive to each other.

If you are a husband whose wife is uninterested in your physical relationship, start praying the scripture that says that a wife's desire shall be unto her husband. (Gen. 3:16.) If you are a wife and your husband is uninterested, start praying the scripture that says he will be ravished always with your love. (Prov. 5:19.) It will work.

Proverbs, chapter 5, says to stay away from a "strange" woman. That kind of relationship, no matter who is to blame, is bad. Don't go that route!

> *For the lips of a strange woman drop as an honeycomb, and her mouth is smoother than oil: but her end is bitter as wormwood, sharp as a two-edged sword.*

> *Her feet go down to death; her steps take hold on hell.*

> *Lest thou shouldest ponder the path of life, her ways are moveable, that thou canst not know them.*
>
> Proverbs 5:3-6

Her mouth is full of flattery: "You look great. You have the biggest muscles. I just love your eyes." Stay away from such a woman.

> *Remove thy way far from her, and come not nigh the door of her house: lest thou give thine honour unto others, and thy years unto the cruel:*

> *Lest strangers be filled with thy wealth; and thy labours be in the house of a*

*stranger; and thou mourn at the last, when
thy flesh and thy body are consumed.*
Proverbs 5:8-11

Solomon paints a clear picture of a man getting involved in illicit relationships. Such a woman usually loves money, and she will bleed her victim to death. She will take everything the man has and leave him broke. She wants his house, his car, his bank account — everything.

Another type of woman mentioned in Proverbs is called a *whore*. (Prov. 23:27.) This is the type of woman who will give her body for any amount; she is just trying to get by. There is also a woman called an *adulteress*. (Prov. 6:26.) She is a married woman who is just looking for a little excitement outside her marriage. She is really not in it for money — just a little excitement and diversion. All three of these women are involved in getting a man outside his marital relationship.

Solomon speaks of the time . . . *when thy flesh and thy body are consumed* (Prov. 5:11). This refers to venereal diseases. They were around then, and they are still here today. They have never been conquered, and I don't think they will ever be cured, because that is part of the wages of sin.

The way to avoid the wages of sin is to be aware of the devices of the enemy. Proverbs 7 reveals some of these devices:

My son, keep my words, and lay up my commandments with thee.

Keep my commandments and live; and my law as the apple of thine eye.

Bind them upon thy fingers, write them upon the table of thine heart.

Say unto wisdom, Thou art my sister; and call understanding thy kinswoman:

That they may keep thee from the strange woman, from the stranger which flattereth with her words.

Proverbs 7:1-5

One of the main things the Devil will use to entrap a man is flattery from a woman. In another place, the Bible speaks of a woman's using her eyelashes, batting them around. (Prov. 6:25.) So remember, the mouth and the eyes have it!

Verses 6 through 21 of this chapter give a graphic description of the entanglement of a foolish young man with an adulterous woman. This strange woman is at her door looking down the street, and she spies a naive young fellow approaching. She then sets out to draw him into an illicit affair. Let's look at the wiles this seductress uses to entice her victim.

First, she watches for him. Nervous and full of energy, she is out looking for a victim. Then she catches him and kisses him — that's the shock treatment! He didn't even know her. She just grabs him and kisses him. Then she says:

> *I have peace offerings with me; this*
> *day have I paid my vows* (v. 14).

That sounds kind of spiritual. "I've just been to church and took communion, and I've done everything the Lord wants me to do. I think He wants me to have a good time now, and you too."

Sometimes people say to me, "Marilyn, I don't believe people can be spiritually deceived into adultery." Yes, they can. I've seen Christians get caught up in adultery and then say, "God told me to do it." God never says that!

The strange woman also uses flattery:

> *Therefore came I forth to meet thee,*
> *diligently to seek thy face, and I have found*
> *thee* (v. 15).

"I've been looking for you and I finally found you. I've been noticing you walking along, and I've been interested in you for a long time." She really wasn't! She had been in and out of that door looking for just anyone! To that kind of woman, no one is special. The only thing special about that young man was his wallet.

Then she begins to paint a sensuously appealing picture of her room and her bed:

I have decked my bed with coverings of tapestry, with carved works, with fine linen of Egypt. I have perfumed my bed with myrrh, aloes, and cinnamon (vv. 16,17).

And just in case he is afraid that her husband might be around, she removes that fear by telling him that her mate is gone on a long trip:

Come, let us take our fill of love until the morning: let us solace ourselves with loves. For the goodman is not at home, he is gone a long journey (vv. 18,19).

"Don't worry about anything. No one will catch you, and no one will know the difference."

Look at how she won him over. It was her fair speech. She caused him to yield with the flattery of her lips. The Bible says, *A man that flattereth his neighbour spreadeth a net for his feet* (Prov. 29:5). Women should be as aware of this device as men.

I know of a minister's wife who was not in a Spirit-filled circle. She shared with me what happened in her marriage. It all began with flattery. A man in their church began to tell her how beautiful she looked. She was an attractive woman, a real knockout, and he would say, "My, you should always wear blue. It looks so good on you."

One morning he called her when it was raining (her husband was out of town). "You don't have to go out to your car in the rain. We'll pick you up. Get an umbrella and be ready. I don't want you to damage your hairdo. You always look so pretty."

Her husband was a conservative Englishman and would never say such things to her. The woman was enjoying hearing all those nice compliments, and she was never worried because this man was much older than she was. But the more he flattered her and carried on over her, the more it fed her ego.

She listened to it, and soon she began to feel an attraction to the man.

She became frightened by what she felt, so she went to some Christians for prayer. "Pray for me," she told them, "I feel like the enemy is setting a trap for me." She was honest! The next week the man was transferred to another job out of town, and she never saw him again. She later said to me, "I saw the device of the enemy. He was using flattery."

It could have ended much worse:

> *He goeth after her straightway, as an ox goeth to the slaughter, or as a fool to the correction of the stocks; till a dart strike through his liver; as a bird hasteth to the snare, and knoweth not that it is for his life* (vv. 22,23).

God's Word gives sound advice to prevent such a downfall in verses 24-27:

Hearken unto me now therefore, O ye children, and attend to the words of my mouth.

Let not thine heart decline to her ways, go not astray in her paths.

For she hath cast down many wounded: yea, many strong men have been slain by her.

Her house is the way to hell, going down to the chambers of death.

Don't go where you can be tempted. If you know that a certain place is a temptation to you, stay away from it. Don't say, "Well, I'm just going to find out how strong I am." You'll find out how weak you are! The Bible doesn't say, "Don't go near temptation." It says, "Flee temptation!" (2 Tim. 2:22.) Look at the hell behind the temptation, and stay away from it. Don't even think about it. Guard your mind. Keep your mind on the Word.

This wasn't the case, however, with that pastor's wife. They took a church in another town. There was a man in the new church, a deacon, with whom they began to fellowship. Nothing much was said, but the pastor's wife and the deacon were attracted to each other. Instead of avoiding contact with this man to whom she was attracted, the woman began inviting him and his wife over for dinner. The two couples spent more and more time together. The pastor did not suspect that there was anything between his wife and this deacon.

Eventually, these two became involved physically. The woman finally came to me about it and said, "I've got to talk to someone. I know that what I am doing is wrong." She knew it was wrong, yet she wanted to leave her husband and run off with the deacon.

One day I told her, "I'll tell you who is going to lose in this whole thing — you. You're going to lose your husband, your children, your position in God. And some day you will lose that deacon, because he doesn't really have any respect for you. One of these days he will drop you! Your husband will find out, and you will have nothing!"

We began to stand together on scripture that God would do a miracle in this situation. One night her husband came home and, for some reason, he became suspicious. "Have you been involved with someone?" he asked. When she answered, "Yes," he just fell apart.

He got his gun and headed for the deacon's house, threatening to kill him. His wife was so frightened that she called the deacon's wife and told her, "My husband is coming over to kill your husband!" (That's not good news at one o'clock in the morning!)

When the pastor arrived at the man's house, the deacon sent his wife to the door. She talked to him for awhile and reasoned with him.

That pastor went back home a broken man. He called his parents, the other deacons, the elders of the church, and told them that he was resigning his pastorate because his wife had been committing adultery.

He then told his wife he was willing to forgive her, and that if she still wanted to be his wife, she could be. Somehow they believed God to put their marriage back together. They left town, and today they are again very effective in the ministry. There are still some scars left from that incident, though it doesn't have to be that way.

The woman told me, "Marilyn, I should have known what was happening way back there the first time. If I had just listened to God then, I would never have gotten involved." It was totally through flattery that she was trapped.

Overcoming Temptation

One of the best ways to overcome temptation is to make a covenant as Job did: *I made a covenant with mine eyes: why then should I think upon a maid?* (Job 31:1). The first step is to guard your thought life.

Secondly, realize the consequences of your actions. When you are involved with someone else, you become one flesh with that person.

> *Know ye not that your bodies are the members of Christ? Shall I then take the members of Christ, and make them the members of an harlot? God forbid.*
>
> *1 Corinthians 6:15*

Do you want to be one flesh with a harlot? Adultery is a sin against your body, your own body. You are damaging your own body when you engage in adultery.

Thirdly, don't associate with people who are involved in this kind of activity: *I wrote unto you in an epistle not to company with fornicators* (1 Cor. 5:9). Don't stay around people who are involved in sinful things. You'll begin to have fantasies. That is where sin starts — in fantasy and imagination. When you start to listen and to entertain thoughts, it opens the door to the Devil. Soon you will find yourself saying, "One time isn't too bad." The second time and the third time you will feel guilty, but the fourth and fifth time you won't feel quite so guilty. By the sixth and seventh time, the sin will have hold of you, and you will be unable to stop it.

God has said all along that He desires to give you and me the best. He has promised us that it will last eternally. If you are not experiencing God's best in every area of your life, claim the scripture that will turn that area around for the good. There isn't any problem or lack that God's Word can't take care of in a positive way.

57

Is your wife turned off with you? Start praying the scripture in Genesis that says her desire is to be towards you.

Is your husband turned off with you? Pray the verse in Proverbs that says he is ravished with your love.

God's Word will work in every area and in every relationship. God wants you to have the best **spiritual** relationship, and He wants you to have the best **physical** relationship. Stand upon His Word from this day forward for yourself, your spouse, and all your family.

3
Warming The Nest

One of the best things that parents can do for their children is to develop the right atmosphere in the home, or what I call "warm the nest."

Frequently we find that even though we are Christians and have a good relationship with the Lord, our home situation is not a warm one. Many times both mates are saved, but just because both are born again does not mean that there is a warm family situation. With this in mind, I would like to discuss how to warm your own home life.

If there is anything that Satan likes to do, it is to knock around a Christian home, causing contention and division. Perhaps your home does not have the joy and abundance of life it is supposed to have in Jesus. When the truth comes forth, it brings light into any situation. As the Word goes forth, I believe it will not only bring light into your home life, but it will also help you to help others to warm their nests too!

Responsibility in the Christian Home

One time my daughter Sarah said to me, "Mother, you know at camp this year I went forward because I felt like I didn't have the assurance that I was saved. But I don't want people to know about it because it could look bad on us."

I said to her, "Sarah, I don't care how it looks. The important thing is your relationship to God. It really doesn't matter what other people say. It matters that we please Him; that's the most important thing."

And I believe the same thing about our home relationships. It doesn't matter what people say. It matters whether we please God, and there is only one way to please Him — by faith in His Word.

We must look to what God's Word says about our situation rather than what we see happening around us. Frequently, when everything is going wrong in our family relationships we tend to look for someone to blame. "What's happening in my home?" we ask. "It's my wife! If she weren't such a nag, we'd have good family relationships." Or we say, "It's my husband! If he weren't such a bum, we'd have a marvelous home." Or perhaps, "It's that rebellious son (or daughter) of ours! If it weren't for him, we'd have a peaceful home."

We always like to put the cause of our disharmony in the home on some other member in the family. But the Bible teaches us that **we** set the atmosphere in the home, and we do that by taking the Word of God and praying and confessing it for our home.

You are the one to set the atmosphere in your home — not your mate, not your children, and not the Devil. Don't say, "Well, it's circumstances." **You have power over circumstances!**

Authority of God's Word

In considering our authority over the circumstances of life, there is one man in the Bible we need to examine. He was a centurion in the Roman army. There are nine centurions mentioned in the Scriptures; all of them are found in the Gospels and the book of Acts. Most of them were good, and one of them even saved Paul's life. (Acts 27:43.) The one we are going to consider is the one about whom Jesus said, "This man has the greatest faith I've ever seen. I've found no faith greater than his, not in all of Israel." (Matt. 8:10.)

I was really impressed by this statement because I'm interested in faith. We please God by our faith. Faith can change every situation. Why was this centurion complimented, and what was the key to his great faith?

As a centurion, he was a Roman army officer in authority over a hundred men. He was totally under the authority and discipline of the Roman Empire. He probably didn't select what he ate when he was in the field. He didn't choose where he lived or where he was sent to serve. His salary was probably predetermined; he couldn't bargain and say, "I'll work for the Roman army as a centurion, if I am well paid." All of his major decisions were determined for him by the Roman Empire. He was a man under authority.

The Bible says, however, that this man was a little different from most Romans because he had a great compassion for his slave. The slave was a bond slave, which meant that the centurion owned him outright. When you find a Roman who was concerned about his slave, that is really significant because slaves were generally treated like cattle or property. If one became ill, that was his problem. If he died, he could be easily replaced. His owner certainly didn't spend time or money trying to restore him to health. But this centurion was concerned about his bond slave and sent a message to Jesus about him.

The Israelites really liked this centurion. They said, . . . *he was worthy . . . for he loveth our nation, and he hath built us a synagogue* (Luke 7:5). This centurion was different from other Roman centurions because most of them were not interested in Israel's God. The fact that this one would build a synagogue for Jehovah really revealed something about what kind of man he was. There was a tenderness in him. When his bond servant became ill, he sent a message to Jesus which said:

> *I am not worthy that thou shouldest come under my roof: but speak the word*

only, and my servant shall be healed.
Matthew 8:8

Notice that the people of Israel said, "This man is worthy," but he said of himself, "I'm not worthy." *Worthy* here means "sufficient." He was saying, "My house isn't good enough for You to come to. I'm not sufficient for You to do anything in relationship to me." But he also said something else:

For I also am a man set under authority, having under me soldiers, and I say unto one, Go, and he goeth; and to another, Come, and he cometh; and to my servant, Do this, and he doeth it.
Luke 7:8

The key word the Lord revealed to me in all of this is the word *also.* I had never seen it before. The centurion said, *I* **also** *am a man set under authority.* What was he saying? "Jesus, I know You're under authority; therefore, You can give authority. I have come under authority; therefore, I can give authority."

Jesus was under authority. He said, "The works I do are done by the Father in Me. I ask the Father to tell Me what to speak. Whatever I do, I am under total authority of the Father in Me." (John 5:36; 14:10,11.) Everything that Jesus did lined up totally with the Word of the Father.

Sometimes when I've felt as if I was really moving in faith and confessing the Word, I've questioned why it didn't work. Why didn't it? Then, from this passage in Luke 7, I began to see a key: I was not allowing the Word to be my **total** authority in the situation. The centurion said, "I see Jesus taking the Father as His total authority. His Word is His authority, and He takes nothing else as His authority." Until you make the Word total authority **of** your situation, it is not going to be the total authority **in** your situation.

This is an example of what usually happens. You pray for a daughter who is rebellious. Everything is falling apart in her life. You pray and confess the Word that she is a changed person. Then someone comes along and says, "You know, that girl probably never will amount to anything." Then some relative will say, "She is just like Aunt Jane. She sure takes after her. Too bad you had to have a child like Aunt Jane."

Not only do people tell you such things about your daughter, you yourself begin to see things in her that are not good. You begin to listen to unbelief and to look at circumstances instead of God's Word. You allow something other than God's Word to be the authority in your life. You pray for one thing for your daughter, but you speak and believe something else. You do not remain under the authority of the Word; therefore, the Word isn't working in authority.

The centurion saw in Jesus that He was **under** total authority to the Word of the Father; therefore, He was **in** total authority over every situation. You will never be the authority in any situation until you have come under total authority of the Word for that situation. You must take the Word above what anyone says about Aunt Jane, above what you see physically in your daughter, and above any circumstances.

If you want to move in authority in the Word, if you want to take the Word as authority over circumstances, you yourself must come under the authority of that Word. The Word has to be your total authority.

It was too bad that the Roman centurion was under the authority of the Roman Empire. The head of that authority was Caesar. Caesar was corrupt, and that empire fell apart because the head, the authority, was corrupt. But the Head of our authority is God the Father. The Bible is His Word. Jesus is that Word, and when we come under His authority, we are not under corrupt authority. We are under authority that is pure and clean and holy.

Jesus said, *Heaven and earth shall pass away, but my words shall not pass away* (Matt. 24:35). We come under the authority of the Word in order to use the authority of that Word. When you come under that authority, you will have to ignore many things that people say to you in unbelief. You will have to ignore the circumstances and say, "I'm under the authority of the Word, and the Word is the authority over this situation."

It will work, and that is why Jesus commended the faith of the centurion. We can exercise the same kind of faith over circumstances in our families!

Exercising the Authority of the Word

Family relationships and circumstances can change. Many years ago I went to the dentist because I had stains on my front teeth. They were stained because I was born and raised in the panhandle of Texas. The water there had something in it that hardened teeth. It prevented cavities, but it also caused brown stains. I've never had a cavity or any other kind of trouble with my teeth, but I did have those stains. Every time I smiled I wondered if people were noticing my stained teeth.

One day a dentist was on our "Life for Laymen" telecast. He said to me, "You know, Marilyn, it doesn't look good for you to be on TV and have those stains on your teeth. There is a new liquid enamel that can be put on teeth to cover the stains. You wouldn't need to have caps. I have never used it, but I would be willing to try it on you as an experiment at no cost."

I said, "Okay, let's do it." I went to his office, and we prayed before he put it on. I prayed, "Lord, I don't want any stains showing on my teeth." The dentist put the enamel on, and it stayed on. It worked very well, but about every six months I'd have to go in for him to replace little pieces of it that had chipped off. Once each year he would remove all of it and start over.

One time when I was in for a six month checkup, the dentist said to me, "I've tried this enamel on a number of people, and you're the only one it has worked on." Then one day I was there again, and he said, "Marilyn, I'm not going to put any more enamel on your teeth because something very unusual is happening. Where I can see the tooth under the places where the enamel has broken off, there is no stain. Let's just wait a little while."

Some time later I went in and he removed all of the enamel. Then he said, "I want you to look at yourself in the mirror. Your teeth have never looked better. You have no stains!"

I have written all of this to illustrate a point in regard to marriage. In marriage relationships, there are often stains in the relationship between husband and wife, between parents and children. We often say, "They will never change. They were born that way." But I was "born with" stains on my teeth, and they changed! They changed because I came under the authority of the Word. The Word can be authority even over stains in your marriage or family relationships. Look to God's Word in your family relationships and not at the stains. God is a miracle-working God, and there is nothing in your home that He cannot repair.

It is my continual prayer that God will help me to see that no corrupt communication comes out of my mouth. By "corrupt communication" I mean anything that is anti-Word. Corrupt communication is unbelief about another person's life or situation. As far as I am concerned, when people start talking negatively about others, I don't want to hear it. I don't want to hear about ministries that have fallen, unless we are going to talk about how God's Word is going to change them.

I don't want to hear about how bad your wife is or how mean your husband is or how nasty your children are, unless you are willing to confess the Word with me for them. I don't want to hear such things because we are not going to change people by griping about them.

I have noticed that often about eighty percent of counseling time is spent in total unbelief. Many times when I am counseling someone about a particular problem in the home, I will say, "Let's just confess God's Word for this situation," and the person will say, "Oh, it's too hard! You don't really understand!" And they will run off to find someone who will listen to their complaints and sympathize with them. I will not sympathize, but I will stand on the Word.

Take the authority of the Word in your home situation. Let God's Word be an authority over you, and then God's Word will be the authority over the situation. It cannot fail.

The Power of Positive Confession

The key to creating the warmth and affection you desire in your home is found in the little book of Philemon:

> *That the communication of thy faith may become effectual by the acknowledging of every good thing which is in you in Christ Jesus.*
>
> Philemon 6

Here the word *effectual* means "energetic." The Apostle Paul is saying that it is his prayer that the communication of Philemon's faith might become **energetic.** How do you make your faith energetic? *By the acknowledging of every good thing which is in you in Christ Jesus.* How do you acknowledge it? With your mouth. You **say** it.

The answer to your home situation is found in your positive confession through faith of the authority of God's Word over that situation. You cannot look at the situation in the natural. You must look at it in the supernatural. When you gripe and complain and criticize family members, you destroy your love for them and wreck your faith, because faith works by love.

However, if you begin to confess what God's Word says about your home life and your family members, you will begin to see that nothing is impossible because you come under the authority of the Word. You will begin to see those family members change. The Word will change them.

This word translated "communication" is the Greek word *koinonia*, which means "fellowship" or "communion." In the fellowship of our faith there is a communion. Fellowship is not only that we believe for ourselves, but that we also believe for others of our household. It is unity.

This is the word Paul used when he wrote to the Romans:

> *For it hath pleased them at Macedonia AND Achaia to make a certain contribution [koinonia] for the poor saints which are at Jerusalem.*
>
> *Romans 15:26*

This was a community project and *koinonia* referred to a collecting of money. Some people say, "I have faith that five or six people who have money can give," but that is not God's way. Paul took a collection from **everyone** on his missionary journeys. It was *koinonia*, a communion of faith. When we begin to energize our faith, it must be a community of faith — all of us moving together in a common faith.

Koinonia not only means a collection of money as a body, but also a "partnership in business," or a "fellowship." When Paul says that the communication of your faith becomes energetic, he is saying that this community should be involved in giving, in partnership, and in fellowship in the home.

To have energetic faith within a home, there must be a giving, one to another. There must be a sharing one with another of ourselves, of our finances, of whatever we have. It must be a partnership. We are united in this. We confess the same thing. We say the same words. We confess the same scriptures as a body. There develops a fellowship in that faith, and it energizes and begins to work.

You may be thinking, "Well, my mate isn't a Christian," or "One of my children isn't serving the Lord." Perhaps none of your children are serving the Lord. How can you have energetic faith in those situations? You can begin to acknowledge what God wants your family to be. You can confess: . . . *the seed of the righteous shall be delivered* (Prov. 11:21), and . . . *all thy children shall be taught of the Lord; and great shall be the peace of thy children* (Is. 54:13). You can begin to make your faith effectual for your household by saying what God's Word says about them.

You may be thinking, "I don't see that. It looks just the opposite in my family." Remember, the Bible doesn't say that faith is what you **see.** Faith is what you **don't see.** It is looking beyond what you see to the invisible One and the promise of the Word of God, and saying what the Word says.

There is a difference between **believing for** your household and **having faith** for your household. When you believe for your household, you say, "Someday my husband will be a Christian. Someday my children will serve the Lord. Someday my wife will be saved. Someday she'll be filled with the Holy Spirit." That's believing.

But we want to enter into more than just believing. We want to have faith, and faith says that it isn't "someday." The Bible says, *Now faith is the substance of things hoped for, the evidence of things not seen* (Heb. 11:1). If you want to enter into faith for your household, you will have to say that it is done **now,** and not "someday." Every day that you confess the Word you are acknowledging it with your mouth. You say, "Thank You, Lord, that now my household is saved, because I have prayed and I have received that for which I have prayed according to Mark 11:24." That is the point at which your faith becomes energized.

It is wonderful when a household can all say the same thing and confess the same things together. Don Gossett told me about one of his sons and how this worked for him. Don has five children. Every morning he and his wife and all five children confess certain scriptures together. As they made these confessions of the Word together, they were making their faith effectual.

While one of the sons was saying these things, he was out using his musical talents to sing with a rock-and-roll band in a nightclub, and using drugs on the side. He was really in the middle of it all, and the parents had no idea what was going on. He was praying with the family in the morning, saying all the right things, then sneaking around at night. Finally Don heard about it. He said that his faith could have been shattered to the ground, but he knew that the Word had been sown and that it had to come up.

One night he walked into the club while his son was singing, walked right up to him at the microphone, and said, "Come with me." Right in front of the whole nightclub! The boy was so shocked that he followed his dad. Don said that for six weeks they had a spiritual battle, but God won out. He won because they made their faith effectual. They had sown and confessed the Word, and the Word came through. His son traveled with the Living Sound Gospel group for a period of time.

As we say that we have received according to Mark 11:24, we make that faith energetic. There are tons of promises for the household, but if you don't say them, you don't make your faith effectual. You make it effectual by saying it — by acknowledging it with your mouth.

73

Warming Your Nest

Here is a scriptural technique for warming your nest:

The first step is for **you** to **make the communication** (the fellowship, the embracing) **of your faith for your household effectual** (energetic) **by acknowledging who everyone in your household is in Jesus Christ.**

Every member of your household who is born again is a begotten one, a saint. You need to acknowledge that fact by your confession and by the way you treat them. You need to treat them with respect. I'm not saying that you shouldn't discipline your children, or that they shouldn't do the dishes or pick up their clothes; but you shouldn't talk to them in a condescending way to get it done.

The second step is for **you** to **identify with your family members.** In his letter to Philemon, Paul refers to one of his disciples, Onesimus, as his son:

> . . . *my son Onesimus, whom I have begotten in my bonds: which in time past was to thee unprofitable, but now profitable to thee and to me: whom I have sent again: thou therefore receive him, that is, mine own bowels.*
>
> *Philemon 10,12*

Paul obviously had a strong affection for Onesimus. He called him his son, his bowels, himself.

74

He identified totally with him. Do the same for your loved ones. Identify with them. Become totally one with them.

The third step is for **you** to **acknowledge and appreciate the worth of your family members.** Onesimus was a runaway slave of Philemon's whom Paul had met and led to the Lord. The name *Onesimus* means "profitable." Here Paul writes to Philemon that while Onesimus was once an unprofitable slave and a thief, now he is truly profitable both to Paul and to his master Philemon.

Did you know that your children were profitable? Not only profitable to the Lord, but also profitable to you! Sometimes I think that the sweetest lessons in faith that I have learned have come from my children.

One time our family was confessing together and releasing our faith for a particular thing to take place. We had confessed this event for a whole month. Finally one day my son Mike walked up to me and said, "Mother, where is that thing we have confessed for?"

I was glad to hear that he was interested, so I told him, "We didn't say it was to be here by the first of the month, but by the end of the month."

"Oh," he said, "then we are still expecting it."

"We are receiving it," I said.

Begin to have your family confess things together with you, and you will find that they are profitable.

The final step is for **you** to **express confidence in your family members.** Did you ever say to your mate or your children, "I have confidence in you. You'll do well"? That is such a key thing. That is making your faith effectual by acknowledging what your household is in Christ Jesus. If anyone ever taught me that by a visual aid, it was my mother.

I can remember coming home from school when I was in the first grade and saying, "Oh, Mother, I'd really like to get all A's on my spelling tests, but I don't know if I can." She'd say, "Of course, you can. I know you can." I remember thinking, *If my mother thinks that, then I must be able.* Throughout my school years whenever I'd go to her all "up-tight" and say, "Mother, I don't know if I can handle this," she would always say, "Of course, you can. I know you can. You've always done well, and you always will." I used to think that she was prejudiced, but now I know she was moving in faith!

There was a specific time in college when I could have gotten into deep sinful difficulties, and I almost did. The night that I was involved in this thing, something happened and I didn't get caught up in it. Two weeks later when I was home I told my mother about it. I was nineteen at the time. I said,

"Mother, I feel like I've let you down. You've always had such confidence in me."

"Marilyn," she replied, "that doesn't bother me anymore than if you had said you hurt your little finger. I still have confidence in you."

You don't know what that did for me! Her confidence in me kept me out of trouble many times when I could have easily gotten into it.

Later on, Mother asked me what time it was that this temptation had come. Then without waiting for my answer, she asked, "At such-and-such a time on Friday night?"

"Yes," I said.

She then told me, "The Lord woke me that night and told me to get out of bed. I prayed in the spirit for you."

She made her faith effectual by acknowledging what God had in me. You can do the same thing by acknowledging what God has in your children and your mate.

What do you confess for your mate? "Aw, that bum! Always grouchy; always nasty! Steady disposition — always hateful!" Or do you confess who your family members are in Christ Jesus and who He is in them? Remember, faith is **not** what you **see.** Faith is what you **know** to be true from the Word.

I have noticed that as I have confessed the Word about my son and my daughter, they have begun to act upon my confession. Mike is a wise son, a totally committed man of God. Sarah is a wise daughter, and she pleases her father.

You might say, "Marilyn, do you always see that?" No, I don't see it with the natural eye all the time, but that's when I confess it the most! Make your faith effectual by acknowledging every good thing that God has in your household. You'll warm your nest and change it from being a cold, indifferent situation into a victorious, harmonious place of peace and joy.

Our nests should be the warmest — the best! I think that Christian mates should have the best relationship of all. Did Jesus come to give us a life of disaster? Or did He come to give us life in abundance? The last verse of Malachi says that in the last days the Lord *shall turn the heart of the fathers to the children, and the heart of the children to their fathers* (Mal. 4:6). We need to quote that for our families and make it effectual.

Covenant Confession

I would like for you to be willing to make a covenant with God about your mouth. Your mouth can work the best for you or it can work the worst for you. *Death and life are in the power of the tongue* (Prov. 18:21). I would like for you to make a covenant that you are not going to allow any corrupt communication to come out your mouth; that you are not going to destroy, you are going to build.

I'm talking about at home first, and then in the rest of the family relationship of the Body of Christ. You can tell me what is wrong with your family members, and they can tell me what is wrong with you, but neither of those is going to change anything — except to make things worse.

Jesus has never called us to criticize; He has called us to edify, to build up. If you sincerely want to see your family and home life changed and transformed by the Word, then make this prayer confession with me:

Father, I know that the power of life and death is in my tongue; Your Word says so. I know that I am an instrument either to build or to destroy.

Right now I enter into a covenant with You that no corrupt communication is going to come out my mouth against my mate, against my children, or against the Church which is the Body of Christ. I am going to live to edify and to build, not to destroy.

Your Word says that I quench every fiery dart that the enemy fires against me by my faith. I take the Word of faith, and I put out the fire of the Devil right now. There is no weapon formed against my home, against my relationship with my mate or my children that shall prosper. Every weapon shall go

down, in the name of Jesus. I thank You that it is my heritage to put down weapons of the enemy, to put down tongues of condemnation, for righteousness is of the Lord.

I am the righteousness of God right now. Thank You for our warm nest that produces the best people who are totally committed to You. In Jesus' name, Amen.

4

Unconditional Love

In the relationship which we experience with our mates and our children, we must have unconditional love. When I think of unconditional love in the New Testament, the person who comes to mind is the father of the prodigal son. (Luke 15:11-32.) This man never cut the string of love. His son wanted all of his inheritance. He left home and moved far away, wanting nothing to do with father and older brother. He wanted all contacts cut, so he cut them!

However, there was one thing that was impossible for this young man to sever, and that was his father's love. When he had lost everything, the son said to himself, *I'm going home.* And he never doubted that his father would receive him. The reason he came home was because of the cord of love. It always succeeds. The Bible says that love never fails. (1 Cor. 13:8.) When we think of love, we want to think of unconditional love — love that is more than an emotion.

Paul says in Ephesians 5:25, *Husbands, love your wives.* And in Titus we are told that older women should teach younger women to love their husbands. (Titus 2:3,4.)

Many times people don't like to hear such teaching because it seems to be "old hat." They tend to think, "Yes, yes, I know I should love my husband, but if you had to live with him, you wouldn't love him either." Or, "If you lived with my wife, you'd move out. You don't know what I have to put up with."

Loving by Faith

One day the Lord began to deal with me about love. In the fifth chapter of Ephesians the Bible says that love is not a condition of the emotions. It is not conditioned upon a person's reaching a certain level of achievement so that they can become worthy of receiving our love. I began to study the life of Jacob and his two wives, and the Lord pointed out to me something about true love.

If you remember, Jacob loved Rachel. He was absolutely wild about her the first time he saw her. (Gen. 29:9-11.) It was love at first sight. If you don't believe in love at first sight, you don't totally believe the Bible! Jacob worked for her for seven years so he could marry her, and it seemed only a day to him because he was so much in love with her. Then, on his wedding night, he had quite a shock! He didn't get Rachel, he got her sister Leah! He hadn't wanted Leah at all; but Laban, Rachel's father, said, "Well, it's our custom to give the older daughter first. If you'll work another seven years, you can have Rachel also." (vv. 21-30.)

Jacob got Rachel within the week, but he had to work another seven years to pay for her. I had never felt that he was obligated to love Leah. *After all,* I thought, *he was stuck with her.* He hadn't wanted her to begin with, so why should he have to love her? Then I began to study in the Book of Genesis, and it says that Rachel's womb was closed up because God saw that Leah was hated and Rachel was loved. (v. 31.) I thought, *So what! Why shouldn't Jacob hate Leah? He never wanted her. When he got stuck with her, naturally his feelings would be even worse.*

Every time he looked at her, he probably thought, *To think! I had to work fourteen years because of you, just so I could have Rachel.* But God was not pleased with that attitude. He said, "Because you love Rachel, and you don't love Leah as you should, Rachel isn't going to have any children." As you read the story, you will notice that something began to happen in Rachel's life. There is an element of faith that came into the life of Rachel and Jacob.

Rachel came to Jacob and said, "Jacob! Give me children or I die!"

Then it says that Jacob was upset with her. (It sounds like their first family quarrel.) "Who do you think I am? God? Do you think it's up to me to give you children?'' Jacob asked her. (Gen. 30:1,2.) Then the Bible says that Rachel prayed, and she did have a child whom she named Joseph. (vv. 22-24.)

Something must have happened to get to this point. Jacob's attitude toward Leah must have changed for Rachel's womb to have been opened. God had evidently dealt with Jacob about loving Leah. He probably didn't love her by his emotions. He didn't love her because she was such a beauty. He didn't love her because she was such a marvelous cook, or because she was a good mother. He loved her simply because God told him to love her, and he did it by faith.

So Leah was loved and Rachel had a son. After Rachel had Joseph, I'm sure she wanted another child. She did have another baby, and his name was Benjamin. But Rachel died giving birth to him.

What happened to Jacob? The Bible says that when he died, he was not buried with Rachel. He was buried with Leah because he loved her. (Gen. 49:29-33.) When he started acting by faith, his emotions followed.

Love is not conditional on your emotions. You do not love a person because they are sweet to you. **Love,** in the Bible, **is an act of faith.** When you act in faith, you will notice that your emotions begin to go with it. Love has a great deal to do with faith, because faith works by love. Faith is unconditional.

The Bible says that you can have anything you believe for: *All things are possible to him that believeth* (Mark 9:23). If faith is unconditional and love goes with it, then love is also unconditional.

Unconditional Love

Now let's look at unconditional love. I want to give you the entire background for this story and for this act of unconditional love. It starts in 2 Samuel 21:1:

> *Then there was a famine in the days of David three years, year after year; and David inquired of the Lord. And the Lord answered, It is for Saul, and for his bloody house, because he slew the Gibeonites.*

Why would David inquire about the famine? God had said in Deuteronomy that as long as Israel served Him, He would bless them. He would bless their crops, their fruit trees, their animals, their families. As long as they kept His Word, He would bless them and bless them and bless them! (Deut. 28:1-14.)

But there was also a curse for disobedience: "But when you don't keep My Word," God had said, "I'm going to make the heavens like brass and the earth like iron, and you are not going to get anything in the way of rain. Your crops will be spoiled if you do not obey Me." (vv. 15-68.)

If you had one year of famine, you might think it was just a natural phenomenon, and two years of famine would surely cause you to wonder. But three years of famine in a tiny nation like Israel would be disastrous. When there were three years without rain, David prayed and asked God, "What is wrong? Have we sinned? Is that why it isn't raining?"

God answered, "Yes, you have sinned. This famine is because of the bloody act of the household of King Saul — because he killed the Gibeonites."

Now let's look at the ninth chapter of Joshua to find out who the Gibeonites were. They were deceivers. These were the people who had come to Joshua when the children of Israel were on their way into the Promised Land. Wearing old clothes and long beards, carrying moldy bread and wineskins, the Gibeonites came to Joshua and said, "We have come from a long way off. We don't live here. We want to make a covenant with you that you will accept us and not fight against us, but rather that you will fight for us. We will be your people under this covenant." (vv. 3-16.)

Joshua made the covenant with these Gibeonites and he should not have done it because God had said for the children of Israel not to make any covenants with the people of Canaan. But Joshua didn't know they lived there. He thought they were from far away as they had said. Three days later he learned the truth, and he said, "You Gibeonites have deceived me!" (v. 22.) But he remained faithful to his covenant and the Gibeonites were allowed to live unharmed among the children of Israel.

But many years later Saul became king. He was very zealous for God some of the time, but at other times he was very unstable. One time he decided that God had told him to wipe out the Hivites and all the Canaanites. He became angry at the Gibeonites and had a large number of them put to death. Saul should not have done that because the Israelites had a covenant with these people, and he broke it. So God said to David, "Until you cleanse the land of the shedding of this innocent blood, there will be a famine." The reason for this is found in Numbers 35:33:

> *So ye shall not pollute the land wherein ye are: for blood it defileth the land: and the land cannot be cleansed of the blood that is shed therein, but by the blood of him that shed it.*

The land could not be cleansed except by the shedding of the blood of the murderer. Otherwise the land was cursed. God was saying to David, "You are not going to have rain until you deal with this matter."

David, knowing this, went to the Gibeonites:

> *Wherefore David said unto the Gibeonites, What shall I do for you? and*

> wherewith shall I make the atonement,
> that ye may bless the inheritance of the
> Lord?
>
> *2 Samuel 21:3*

David was saying, "We're not going to have rain until this issue is settled. How are we going to settle it?" They couldn't kill Saul because he was already dead. The Gibeonites were very spiritual people; therefore, they said, *We will have no silver nor gold of Saul, nor of his house* (v. 4). In other words, "We aren't in this for money." They could have demanded money, but they only wanted what was right.

> And they answered the king, The man
> that consumed us, and that devised against
> us that we should be destroyed from
> remaining in any of the coasts of Israel,
>
> Let seven men of his sons be delivered
> unto us, and we will hang them up unto the
> Lord in Gibeah of Saul, whom the Lord did
> choose. And the king said, I will give them
> (vv. 5,6).

David, however, spared Mephibosheth, the son of Jonathan the son of Saul, *because of the Lord's oath that was between them, between David and Jonathan the son of Saul* (v. 7). A covenant existed between David and Jonathan that they would take care of each other's children.

"You can't have Mephibosheth," David said, "but there are two sons of Rizpah you may have."

Rizpah was Saul's widow. Her name means "a hot stone." It is her story of unconditional love that I want to share with you. It will warm your heart. She was a beautiful woman, and Saul made her his concubine after defeating her father in battle. Saul was physically attracted to her, and they ended up having two sons. Later when Saul was killed, his military leader, Abner, took her for his own.

Abner was also killed, leaving Rizpah twice a widow. She lost both Saul and Abner, and she had only two sons left. These two sons are among the seven men that were turned over to the Gibeonites for the sin of Saul:

> But the king took the two sons of Rizpah the daughter of Aiah, whom she bare unto Saul, Armoni and Mephibosheth; and the five sons of Michal the daughter of Saul, whom she brought up for Adriel the son of Barzillai the Meholathite:
>
> And he delivered them into the hands of the Gibeonites and they hanged them in the hill before the Lord . . . (vv. 8,9).

David took the five grandsons of Saul and the two sons of Rizpah and turned them over to the Gibeonites to be hanged "before the Lord." This was not something that was done in vengeance; it was done "as unto God."

> ... and they fell all seven together, and were put to death in the days of harvest, in the first days, in the beginning of barley harvest (v. 9).

It is very important that you see the timing. Barley harvest occurred in the springtime, about the same time as the day of the Passover. When those men were hanged, it was at barley harvesttime. But there was no harvest! It hadn't rained for three years. Why were their lives taken at harvesttime? Because they were given as an atonement at the Passover as a covering for sins, at the very time that a harvest was needed. In essence, the people were saying, "We are shedding blood to cleanse the land in order to get a harvest." Everything was done in a spiritual way — at the right time, on the right day, in the prescribed manner — all because they wanted to have rain.

Now watch a true display of unconditional love:

> And Rizpah the daughter of Aiah took sackcloth, and spread it for her upon the rock, from the beginning of harvest until water dropped upon them out of heaven, and suffered neither the birds of the air to rest on them [the seven bodies] by day, nor the beasts of the field by night (v. 10).

Notice that she didn't, wear the sackcloth as they usually did. She spread it out on the rock. Evidently she put it up like a tent over her head in the daytime and used it as a cover for warmth at night. She stayed out there from the beginning of harvest until water dropped upon them from heaven.

Rizpah said, "I'm going to stay here until it rains." Why would she do that? She suffered neither the birds of the air to rest on those bodies, nor the beasts of the field. Why? Because only criminals or ungodly men were thrown to the animals.

If you go through the Old Testament, you will notice that whenever God was really passing judgment upon a person, He would say, "And the beasts of the field shall eat your flesh." Jezebel was a good example of God's severe judgment. She was pushed out a window and the dogs ate her flesh. (2 Kings 9:32-37.) It was always a great curse for a person's body to be left to the animals; it meant that the person didn't belong to Jehovah-God.

By staying out there and protecting those bodies, Rizpah was saying, "I don't want my children's bodies to be eaten by animals. I want them to belong to Jehovah-God. I want them to have a proper burial. I know they did wrong, but I'm going to stand up for them." She stayed out there and drove away the birds all day long, and at night she built a fire to keep the animals away. When she was cold, she took the sackcloth and wrapped it around herself (like a mourning cloth) to keep herself warm.

Some of us might have stood that for a couple of days, but Rizpah did it for five months! Day and night she protected those bodies. Why did she love them like that — even when they probably didn't deserve such love? She loved them unconditionally.

Kinds of Love

There are four kinds of love.

First, there is *eros*, from which we get our word *erotic*. There is nothing wrong with physical love except when it gets out of the boundaries of what God's Word says it should be. It is a love that we should have, particularly between husband and wife. If you don't think there is physical love between husband and wife in the Bible, you should read Proverbs 5:19 which says, *Be thou ravished always with her love*. In Genesis 3 the Bible says that a woman's desire will be to her husband, which means that she will long after him. (v. 16.) That has to do with physical love. And, of course, the New Testament says that the marriage bed is pure and undefiled. (Heb. 13:4.)

The second kind of love is *phileo* love. This kind of love is reciprocal love. It is love between husband and wife, between friends, between family members, between parents and children. It is love based on giving and receiving one with another. Often it has been referred to as "brotherly love" or "fraternal love."

The third kind of love is *storge* love. This is family love — the kind of love you have for aunts, uncles, nieces, nephews, and cousins. Some people are just wild about their relatives. One Thanksgiving we had seventeen people come and stay with us in our home for three days. My husband invited all those relatives. We had a house full, and he loved every minute of it! I've always said that he must have gotten an extra portion of *storge* love. It is a good kind of love.

The fourth kind of love is *agape* love. This is the kind of love that gives and doesn't expect anything in return. It has no strings attached. It is the God-kind of love, the kind of love that God displayed when He *so loved the world that he gave his only begotten Son* (John 3:16).

Many people take the Name of His Son and curse it and damn it, but He still loves them even though they don't love Him back. He sends the rain and sunshine on the sinner as well as the saint. Why? Because He loves them. *We love him, because he first loved us* (1 John 4:19). He loves us even if we don't love Him back. That's unconditional love!

Rizpah loved unconditionally. She said, "I love my boys, even though they have nothing to give to me.

I love them, and I want them to have a decent burial.
I'm staying here until something is done, until the
curse is lifted. I'll stay here until it rains." And she
stayed five months!

> *And it was told David what Rizpah the*
> *daughter of Aiah, the concubine of Saul,*
> *had done.*

> *And David went and took the bones of*
> *Saul and the bones of Jonathan his son*
> *from the men of Jabesh-gilead, which had*
> *stolen them from the street of Beth-shan,*
> *where the Philistines had hanged them,*
> *when the Philistines had slain Saul in*
> *Gilboa:*

> *And he brought up from thence the*
> *bones of Saul and the bones of Jonathan his*
> *son; and they gathered the bones of them*
> *that were hanged.*

> *2 Samuel 21:11-13*

After five months the flesh was decayed and
gone. Only the bones were left, but no dog dragged
off any of them. They were all there because Rizpah
stayed up all night protecting them and seeing that
nothing happened to them.

Some might call that ghoulish, but God says it is
love. Sometimes people who are unconditional in
their love are called crazy by the world.
Unconditional love can only be from God because we

don't have it in the natural. That's why I know something must have happened in Rizpah's spirit. It takes the supernatural to bring about *agape* love. The Bible says that God's love is shed abroad in our hearts by the Holy Spirit. (Rom. 5:5.) The more of the Spirit you receive, the more love you will experience in your life.

When David heard of all that went on with Rizpah and her sons, he gathered up all the bones and buried them in the country of Benjamin in Zelah:

> And the bones of Saul and Jonathan his son buried they in the country of Benjamin in Zelah, in the sepulchre of Kish his father: and they performed all that the king commanded. And after that God was intreated for the land (v. 14).

It finally rained. Why didn't it rain before the bones were buried? What are a bunch of bones to God anyway? A bunch of bones showed the love of a concubine, a Philistine named Rizpah who wouldn't let go of her sons until they were buried as unto Jehovah. She wouldn't let go, and God saw and honored that faith until those bones got a proper burial. When they had been buried, God sent the rain. He didn't send the rain first, then have them bury the bones. He did it the other way. Until David moved and did the right thing in burying them, God wasn't going to send rain to bless the land. The blood had been shed, the land had been cleansed, and there was a woman who wouldn't let go of God.

Did you know that you can hold onto God and hold onto His Word until He cannot do anything until that Word is fulfilled?

The story of Lot illustrates this point. Do you remember what the angel told Lot in Sodom? He said, "Get out because I can't do anything here until you leave." (Gen. 19:22.) Abraham had prayed and entreated God to spare the city for the sake of a few righteous ones, and he knew that his nephew Lot and his family were down there. God could not pour out His wrath on Sodom and Gomorrah until Lot had left. That's what faith in the Word of God will do.

Remember at the beginning I told you that Rizpah means "hot stone"? (Don't you think her story warms your heart?) We were in the Louvre Museum in Paris one Christmas and there was a huge painting of Rizpah in one of the galleries. I don't know who painted it, but it is the most gorgeous picture to me because I know the story so well. The painting shows the woman out on a rock whipping something in the breeze (the sackcloth). It shows the bodies there too. It is a life-sized picture of this woman in whom there was such love, such reaching out. You can see that she isn't going to stop until this thing is accomplished. The artist captured all the feelings of Rizpah. When you look at that picture, especially if you are a mother, you are warmed by it.

But remember, Rizpah went beyond mother love — she went into *agape* love. Mother love can fail. Have you ever been so angry with your children that you weren't sure sometimes if you loved them? But did you ever notice that God's love could come upon the scene and you could love them when they were unlovely?

Loving Unconditionally

Unconditional love is also shown in the story of Hosea. He loved with an unconditional love. He just plain loved! He married a woman named Gomer who was an adulteress, a prostitute. She straightened up for a while after they were married. They had a son, Jezreel, and everything was sweet. Jezreel means "God has planted you."

Then a second child came, but in the meantime Gomer had become restless and had begun to step out a bit. I don't even think the second child belonged to Hosea; I believe the father was someone Gomer ran around with because God called this child Loruhamah, which means "I won't have mercy on you." (Whenever you see "lo" in front of a name in the Bible, it means "not.")

Hosea still didn't give up on Gomer. We would have said, "Throw her out! She's no good. She's just trash." But not Hosea. Then Gomer became pregnant again, and Hosea didn't think that this was his child either. I don't think Gomer even knew for sure herself. This child was named Lo-ammi, meaning "You are not mine."

After their third child was born, Gomer left Hosea with the children and ran off to have fun. Hosea said to the children, "Jezreel, go talk to your mama. Ruhamah, go talk to your mama and tell her to come home. You, too, Ammi." (Hos. 2:1.) There are no "lo's" here because Hosea stood in faith for his children, and the Word says that one believing mate can sanctify the whole household. (1 Cor. 7:14.) Many people say, "If only my mate would believe." But one is enough to sanctify the house!

The children went to their mother and begged her to come home. However, adultery and new wine take away the heart for natural affection. (Hos. 4:11.) Those poor, pitiful-looking little children went to their mother and said, "Mother, please come home. We hate Daddy's cooking!" Wouldn't that touch you? But it didn't touch Gomer a bit. She couldn't have cared less! She was having "fun."

Hosea never stopped loving Gomer. Love never fails, and faith works by love. If you are trying to work faith without love, it won't work. And neither will love work without faith. If you try to love by feelings and by what you see, you'll run out of love. But God set a wall around Gomer and made her repulsive to her lovers. She probably thought, "What has happened to all my business? No one loves me anymore." God will turn situations around if we do our part and love by faith, not by feelings.

Gomer ended up on a slave block, and Hosea went down to buy her back. We would have said, "Oh, Hosea! Don't buy her back. Hasn't she caused you enough heartache? Leave her there!" But Hosea didn't have any strings on his love. He believed God could put their marriage back together, and because he believed it, he acted on his faith and bought her back. Now, not only was she his wife, she was also his slave. If that had been me, I would have started giving orders and treating her like the slave she was. But Hosea didn't feel that way. He was her master, true, but he told her, "You're not going to call me *Baali* (my master). You are going to call me *Ishi* (my husband)." (Hos. 2:16.)

Hosea said, "I'm going to be so sweet to you that you are going to love me." I would have said she didn't deserve love, but Hosea's love was unconditional — it had no strings attached. God says that the picture of Hosea and Gomer is the same picture of His love for us — He loves us unconditionally. He loves you just as you are, and He is calling you to love by faith, unconditionally.

Sometimes the best time to say "I love you" to someone is when you don't feel like you love them. I have said to my husband, when I was really angry with him, "Do you know that I love you?" And I would think, *But I don't feel it.* But in saying it, the feeling would follow. Did your mate ever do anything really dumb, and you wanted to say to him or her, "That certainly was stupid!" Instead, try saying, "You know, I really love you." **Act by faith and the feeling will follow.**

There was a couple in Amarillo, Texas, with whom we were good friends. They grew up together in the same little town in Texas, just outside Amarillo, and were childhood sweethearts. They fell in love in junior high school and were married right after graduation from high school.

During the Second World War, he worked at a military base, and he supposedly fell in love with a woman who worked there. He came home one day and told his wife that he didn't love her anymore. He wanted to leave her and their little girl.

It absolutely shattered the wife. She later told me that her husband and his new girlfriend moved into the apartment that had been their honeymoon home. It was a terrible thing for her. She would run into that woman when she went downtown. She became physically ill, and her doctor told her she would have to move to another climate. She became bitter about the whole situation, but God began to deal with her attitude. He spoke to her one day and said, "If you had been tempted like Joe was, and you were like him, you would have done even worse."

She began to have faith that her home would come back together. In the meantime the Lord had been dealing with her husband. He left the other woman and went to Hawaii for two years to work in the civil service. All that time he sent back support for her and the little girl, who were then living in Louisiana. Her parents kept telling her that he would never come back to her. "He will never, never be your husband again," they told her. "Forget him! He's no good!"

Her love for him, however, was an unconditional love, and she had unconditional faith. She didn't **feel** love, but she had faith that God would restore her home. At the end of the two years he wrote to her and said, "I'm coming back to the States, and I want to come back to you, if you will have me." Of course, that was the answer to her prayer! But when she saw him, she still had no feelings at all. She told me, "I didn't love him, and I didn't hate him. I felt nothing. Just zero."

One day she prayed, "Lord, if You can return my husband to me, You can return my love for him. I take love for him by faith." She began to say to her husband, "Joe, I love you." And the more she said she loved him, the more she began to feel love for him. The more acts of love she did for him, like polishing his shoes or fixing his favorite meals, the more he responded. "Sometimes," she said, "I felt like saying, 'I don't feel like babying you. **You** should be babying me. You're the one who ran off!' " But she did it anyway, and she did it in faith.

She told me her entire story because I had said to her, "I so admire your marriage. I think you have one of the greatest marriages I've ever seen."

She said, "Let me tell you when it all began. It began when I loved him by faith, unconditionally."

If you are waiting for an emotion, you will never experience God's love. You may experience erotic love, phileo love, or storge love, but you will never experience agape love if you start out loving by your feelings. You experience God's love when you love **by faith.** Paul says in Colossians 3:14 that we are to put on love. You put it on by faith. It isn't just an "act," not if you're doing it in obedience to the Word. Then it's an act of faith.

Sometimes you might be around people who have nasty dispositions. What are you going to do? Put on love! For people who have been real nasty to me, I pray that the Lord will surround them with faith and love. I love them with His love. I love them unconditionally. I've noticed that the more I use the word *love*, the more I begin to experience the love of God for that person.

Pray with me right now. I want first to pray for **you.** Then I want you to pray for someone who is hard for you to love:

Dear Father, I come to You in Jesus' name. I feel that this is such an important moment for the person reading this message. I know that there are

some reading this who have a hard, bitter core in their spirits for certain people. They've repented and said that they have forgiven, but they never have really expected to love that person with Your love. I thank You that the person reading this message has a divine appointment with You to experience Your love.

Now stretch out your arms, palms up, and hold up before the Lord that person whom you find difficult to love. Confess right now by faith that you love that person with God's love. Pray this prayer:

Dear Heavenly Father, I come to You in the name of Jesus. I hold this one before You, and I forgive them and I love them with Your love. I love them by faith. I ask You to bless them and do good to them. I loose them into Your love. Thank You for shedding Your love abroad in my heart. Amen.

5

Handling Parenthood

God has given parents tremendous responsibilities. Along with those responsibilities, however, God has given tremendous power to carry out what He requires. The power God gives to parents is in His Word. I believe that we do not fully understand how powerful the Word is. In Hebrews 1:3 the Bible says that God is **upholding all things by the word of his power.**

When you got up this morning, I doubt seriously that you went out and said, "I wonder if the sun is here today? Maybe it fell." No, you are not worried about that, and you are not worried about the position of the moon either. Why? Because God spoke them there by His Word, and they will stay there by His Word. If the Word can hold the sun and moon in place, then I believe it can answer any need that you and I may have in our families.

Praying the Word

We have been experimentally praying the Word into a lot of different situations. I don't pray anymore unless I pray the Scriptures, and I'll tell you why:

The Word cannot return void. (Is. 55:11.) Our opinion, our idea, of God's will can be all wrong, and if we pray amiss, then we don't receive. If we pray the Word, however, we are planting incorruptible seed. As we pray, it must come up.

My husband and I plant a garden every year, and some years our cucumbers have not come up. I said to him, "What is it with me and cucumbers?"

"Well," he said, "you probably had bad seed."

And I believe we did. But the Word of God is never bad seed. It is incorruptible; it cannot decay. It has to come up, but it doesn't always come up at the time we are expecting it. That is especially true if you plant today and expect it to come up tomorrow.

I have noticed that at times I have prayed over an immediate need, but I did not see the answer until three or four months later. The Lord began to deal with me about this. He said, "It takes time for seed to come up. You don't expect carrots to come up the day after you plant them, do you? Pray now for tomorrow's needs."

I'm learning to plant **now** for what my children will need in the future, perhaps ten years from now. I believe that there is much planting that we can do in praying for our children, our families, and the needs that we will have. That is what I would call "preventative praying." Too many times when we have a big emergency, we enter into "curative praying," which takes much more effort. That can be a very frustrating battle of prayer sometimes! The important thing is to pray the Word **now** for future needs; then when the time comes, you can reap the results.

I began praying the Word for an opening on educational TV two years before our program ever went on the air. After I prayed the Scriptures and claimed it, I did not continue to pray for it, but I did continue to thank the Lord for it every day. Seed needs water! The Bible says that we are to *hold fast the profession* (confession) *of our faith without wavering; for he is faithful that promised* (Heb. 10:23). When we water that seed, I believe that we water it with the confession of our mouths. Every day I thanked God that according to the Word I had my request.

When people talked to me about the TV program, they would say, "I don't think you'll ever be on educational TV." I continued, however, to thank God that we would be. Even the educational station in Denver that I wanted to get our program on told me that it was a dead issue. But I said, "Good! I believe in resurrection!" I thanked God that my TV program was resurrected.

Later on, I was at PTL Network teaching a seminar. One morning when I got up, it just seemed like the enemy came against me especially hard saying, "You will never see that TV program come to pass! Why don't you just forget it? People are going to think you are crazy. You're always talking about it, confessing that you have it, but you don't! It's obvious that you aren't going to get it." Then I thought of another way to water the seed that I had planted — I wrote it down. On the January calendar I wrote, "Thank God, this year I'm on educational TV teaching the Bible."

That afternoon I was interviewed on the daily telecast of the PTL Club, and I shared this with Jim Bakker. He invited both the studio and television audience to pray with us about my plans. I went to teach the afternoon seminar, and a secretary interrupted it to tell me that I had an emergency telephone call from Denver. It was my secretary, and she said, "I know that you don't like to be interrupted, but this is so important that I had to call you. The educational TV channel just called us and wanted to know when you would be back in Denver. They want you to start taping the series for this spring."

Once you plant the seed, you have to keep watering it! If you keep on asking, you aren't moving in faith. You can ask and ask and ask, but never believe you've received. And you don't! Once you have asked, once you have prayed the Word, once you know it is the will of God, then don't ask again, but **do** thank God for it!

There are certain scriptures that I pray every day for my household. For my son and daughter, I pray Proverbs 11:21 which says that *the seed of the righteous shall be delivered.* We live in a very evil day, and there are many things that come against us. The Scriptures say that in the last days there will be perilous times. I pray for my children early in the morning before they go out to meet the day. I pray that they will grow *in wisdom and stature, and in favour with God and man* (Luke 2:52). I pray daily because I know that they need it for each day.

For myself I pray 1 Corinthians 2:16: *But we have the mind of Christ.* Every day I pray, "Thank You, Father, that I have the mind of Christ because that is what Your Word says." Never in the day do I say, "I'm just too dumb to figure that out," or, "I never have done well in this." I **never** say those things because it would refute what I have prayed. That would be digging up the seed and saying, "I don't believe that anymore."

God's Word says that I have the mind of Christ. If I have the mind of Christ, I'm very wise, and you are too! Never again will I say to a Christian, "You're just dumb. You're not catching on to this. You're slow." **Never!** That is an unscriptural statement. Every day I plant the seed of God's Word. I plant it every day because I need it every day. I confess it, and I thank God for it. I believe that I move in it, and I do!

As we pray the Scriptures, our prayers tend to gain momentum. Every day I pray for every person who is reading through the Bible with me, *Open thou mine eyes, that I may behold wondrous things out of thy law* (Ps. 119:18). I pray that scripture every day for every person reading with me, and I pray it early.

One day I said to my husband, Wally, "You know, I've been praying that scripture now every day for over six months, and something is happening to me. Every time I open my Bible I'm getting a revelation. I can't sit down and read the Word without getting a new revelation."

In the past when I would read the Bible, some days it would be great and some days it would be dull. Sometimes I felt that I was just plowing through it and wasn't getting a thing out of it. But I can't say that anymore. There is revelation every time now. And it came from praying the Scriptures for my friends and family.

Plant spiritual seed and you'll reap!

One time I was doing a study on Mephibosheth, but it was really a study on friendship. *Mephibosheth* means "a shameful thing." That's a terrible name to give a child! His father, Jonathan, was a spiritual man, there is no question about that. Why, then, did he call his son Mephibosheth? He didn't! One day as I was reading along, I noticed that the Bible said that when he was born, he was named

110

Merib-baal, which means "he will contend with Baal." He was a man of God who contended with the idolatrous worship of Baal. That is what his father, Jonathan, named him. But later on after Jonathan had died, his nurse dropped him, and he was crippled by the fall. Evidently she began to call him Mephibosheth, which meant, "What a shame," or, "It's shameful that he has broken his feet." (2 Sam. 4:4.) From then on, he was called Mephibosheth. I had not seen that before. It was a revelation to me as I was reading the Word.

I said to myself, "What's happening to me? I get something new every time I'm in the Word."

God said to my spirit, "You know what's happening. You've planted every day. Didn't you think you'd get a harvest?"

If you have been consistently reading through the Bible, and it's beginning to become more alive to you than ever before, it's because you've been planting seeds. You can't plant the Word and not have it come up. You are going to get a harvest, **if** you plant! It gains momentum in your life because the Bible says you go from faith to faith, glory to glory, and strength to strength.

Now let's get into the meat of the Word. God wants His children to have meat. He said that if we just use milk, we are unskillful in the Word. (Heb. 5:13.) Milk is good for starters, but God wants us to have meat. He wants us to use the Word skillfully.

You could read the Bible, know it backwards and forwards, and still never know how to mix it with faith. It would never be profitable to you. If you will take a scripture, however, and begin to pray it and quote it and confess it and stand uncompromisingly on it, you will find that the Word works! **When you begin to get into the Scriptures, you begin to see that there is absolutely nothing impossible to you with the Word of God.**

Take the Word into your family situations. One time I began to pray Proverbs 10:1 for my son: *A wise son maketh a glad father.* I began to confess, "Mike is a wise son and he pleases his father." Mike had never had good grades in school. I was praying that scripture, not particularly with his grades in mind, but that he would make wise decisions. I prayed that he would please his earthly father and his heavenly Father.

Some time later Mike's math teacher called me and, as we were visiting together, said, "My, your son is certainly outstanding in math. He's always been good in math, hasn't he?"

"No, not really. It's always been his poorest subject."

"Really?" the instructor said, "He's good in math. He has quite a bit of talent in that area."

I said to the Lord later, "That was such a shock to me."

"Why?" the Lord replied. "You've been praying that he would be a wise son. What did you expect?"

I guess I didn't expect it in that area. But you see, when you begin to pray the Word, it works in all areas.

If we pray the Word, we should expect to receive what we request in Jesus' name. In Proverbs the Bible says, *the hearing ear, and the seeing eye, the Lord hath made even both of them* (Prov. 20:12). That's what I am going to pray for you right now:

Dear Father, I come to You in the name of Jesus Christ. I ask that You give every person reading this message seeing eyes and hearing ears to receive what You have for them personally. I ask that by the time they have finished reading this book that they will have become so excited about the Word of God that they will become planters and reapers of the bountiful provisions of Your Word.

I pray that Your Word will be sown in each family who comes in contact with this book. And I expect a rich harvest of good things for them. Amen.

Hannah's Prayer

When you plant the Word, it not only affects you, it also affects many other people. The story of Hannah is a good example:

Now there was a certain man of Ramathaim-zophim, of Mount Ephraim, and his name was Elkanah, the son of Jeroham, the son of Elihu, the son of Tohu, the son of Zuph, an Ephrathite:

And he had two wives; the name of the one was Hannah, and the name of the other Peninnah: and Peninnah had children, but Hannah had no children.

1 Samuel 1:1,2

Ramah is really the name of the town that was located north of Jerusalem. It means "a mount of Rama," and it also means "the mount of the watchers." Keep that in mind — it is important.

The problem with these women was that they were both married to the same man. Hannah, whose name means "gracious," was the one who was loved, but she didn't have any children. That's why her husband had taken a second wife. He felt that he had to have children. So he married Peninnah, whose name means "pearl." As you study this story you might think that Peninnah was a thorn, not a pearl, because she was very jealous of Hannah. Peninnah was just a convenience — she bore children. On the other hand, Hannah felt very much "put down" by Peninnah, because she was barren. And she knew that if she were able to have children, Peninnah would not be around any longer.

Peninnah plagued Hannah and picked at her continually because of her barrenness. In those days it was considered a curse for a woman not to have children because God had said in Deuteronomy: "When you go into the Promised Land, I will bless you. I will multiply your children. I will bless the fruit of your womb. I will multiply your fields." (Deut. 28:1-14.) God had promised that He would prosper these people with families — large families — so, if a woman didn't have any children, it was thought that there must be something wrong with her.

And that's exactly what Peninnah was saying to Hannah, especially at the time they all went up to Shiloh to worship once a year:

> And her adversary also provoked her
> sore, for to make her fret, . . . year by year,
> when she went up to the house of the Lord,
> so she provoked her; therefore she wept,
> and did not eat (vv. 6,7).

Once a year they went to worship, and Peninnah would provoke Hannah all the way to "church." Have you ever noticed that you have some of your greatest spiritual battles on Sunday morning? That's typical of the Devil. But if you will bind those battles on Saturday night, you won't have to put up with them on Sunday morning. That's preventative praying. But every year Peninnah gave Hannah a lot of "static."

115

Then said Elkanah her husband to her,
Hannah, why weepest thou? and why
eatest thou not? and why is thy heart
grieved? am not I better to thee than ten
sons? (v. 8).

Elkanah gave more to Hannah than he did to
Peninnah and her children. "Hannah, I love you so
much. Aren't I better to you than ten sons? Must you
have a child? I am so good to you. Can't you forget
this thing of having a baby?" Perhaps she could have
except that Peninnah never let her forget.

That year when they arrived at Shiloh for
worship, Hannah felt she had just come to the end.
She had been provoked for so long and was so
miserable about it that she was ready to throw in the
towel. All that week of worship, when they offered a
peace offering, they would spread a table on the
grounds of the temple and eat part of the offering
they had prepared. The whole family partook, and
they celebrated the fact that they had peace with
God.

When they sat down to eat dinner, Hannah was
too upset and depressed to eat, so she did something
better: She began to pray. When she prayed, she was
extremely sorrowful. She was so sorrowful that she
was moving her lips as she prayed, but no sounds
were coming out of her mouth. Her actions caught
the attention of the priest on duty at the time. His

name was Eli. He saw her as she was praying and thought she was drunk, so he went over to her and said, *How long wilt thou be drunken? put away thy wine from thee* (v. 14).

Of all people to make a statement like that! Eli had two sons name Hophni and Phinehas. Hophni means "my fist," and Phinehas means "a mouth of pity." I call these two the fighter and the whiner. They were really bad news! They were grown men, priests like Eli, but they were bad priests. Their father would never correct them, and they were drunkards and gluttons. They were also adulterers, and they stole from the people.

Here was Eli saying to Hannah, who was travailing in prayer, "Why are you drunk?" And he was not correcting his own sons who were drunk all the time! Hannah could have mentioned that fact to Eli. I don't imagine it was any great secret! But Hannah didn't say that. She was too desperate. She didn't become offended. Instead she answered in a very respectful way:

> *No, my lord, I am a woman of a sorrowful spirit: I have drunk neither wine nor strong drink, but have poured out my soul before the Lord.*
>
> *Count not thine handmaid for a daughter of Belial: for out of the abundance of my complaint and grief have I spoken hitherto* (vv. 15,16).

117

Look what Hannah had prayed:

And she vowed a vow, and said, O Lord of hosts, if thou wilt indeed look on the affliction of thine handmaid, and remember me, and not forget thine handmaid, but wilt give unto thine handmaid a man child, then will I give him unto the Lord all the days of his life, and there shall no razor come upon his head (v. 11).

Hannah said, "Lord, I don't want just a child. I want a boy. If You will give me a boy, I will vow that I will give him to You as long as he lives." You may not think that is anything so super special, but it is. Normally priesthood did not begin until the person was twenty-five years old, and only continued until the age of fifty-five. But Hannah told God, "Lord, if You will give me a son, he will serve You forever. He will never retire." Later we see that she gave her son to the Lord when he was about three years old.

As Hannah was praying, Eli misunderstood and interrupted her. She explained to him that he was wrong, but she never told him exactly what she had been praying. Then Eli said something to her that was excellent counsel. (Don't ever try to make anyone in the Bible all good or all bad because they were just human. You'll find that the best of them had some bad points, and the worst of them had some good points.) Eli spoke a very faith-filled statement to her. He said:

> *Go in peace: and the God of Israel grant thee thy petition that thou hast asked of him* (v. 17).

Eli said, "Hannah, you've got it. Go on home and forget it." That's right in line with the words of Jesus: *What things soever ye desire, when ye pray, believe that ye receive them, and ye shall have them* (Mark 11:24). When do you believe — when you see it or when you pray? You have to believe that you have received it **when you pray.**

Faith isn't what you see — faith is just the opposite. If you see it, it is no longer faith. It is sight. Faith is never what you see. You must believe you receive it when you pray. Eli told Hannah, "You have received it! Go home." And that is good, because she could have kept praying and praying (as I have done sometimes) and prayed herself out of any faith she ever had.

She believed what the priest had said to her. She jumped up, went back, sat down, and ate because she was no longer depressed. It wasn't a long time of praying, evidently, because the meal wasn't finished. She sat down and ate with them, and was happy. Someone might have said, "Well, Hannah, you don't have your baby." But she could say, "Oh, yes, I do! I've got it because God has heard me. I've received it!" She went home, not hoping, not just believing, but in faith that she had received.

> *And they rose up in the morning early,*
> *and worshipped before the Lord, and*
> *returned, and came to their house to*
> *Ramah: and Elkanah knew Hannah his*
> *wife; and the Lord remembered her* (v. 19).

She conceived and bore a child. When the child was born, she called him Samuel. I love this name because there is a play on words in it. It means "asked of God," and it also means "lent to God." Hannah held her baby boy and knew that she had made a vow, and she didn't change her mind when she received him. When she received him, she said, "I asked you of the Lord. That's how I got you, and I've loaned you to the Lord, so I won't have you long. I'll be giving you back to Him."

The next year when Elkanah was going to go up to Shiloh to worship, Hannah said, "I won't be going with you this time because I'm not going until I wean the child. When he is weaned, I'll go, and I'll leave him there." (v. 22.)

When the child was weaned, Hannah went with her husband to Shiloh with their sacrifice, and they took little Samuel with them.

Hannah spoke to Eli, the priest: "Eli, do you remember me? I'm the woman you thought was drunk, and I told you I was praying. You told me to go home, that I had received my request. I want you to know that this is my prayer request." Then she held out the little boy to Eli saying, "He's all yours. I vowed a vow that if the Lord would give me a boy, I would give him to the Lord to serve Him forever."

Eli could have rationalized and said, "But he is so young. God doesn't expect this of you!" But he didn't. Hannah had made a promise to God, and she kept it.

Hannah's Harvest

Hannah left Samuel at the temple, but when she left, she was not depressed. If you had been that mother, wouldn't you have felt a little depressed? "Oh, I don't have any more children! That's the only one I have, and I waited so long to get him. Now I have to tell him good-bye, and I won't see him again until next year." But Hannah didn't say that. In fact, the first ten verses of the next chapter record her prayer of thanksgiving. It is a song of victory. In it she says some things that are very similar to the *Magnificat*, the prayer that Mary made after learning that she was going to become the mother of God's Son. (Luke 1:46-55.)

As Hannah was thus worshiping the Lord, she said something that no one else had ever said. It is a tremendous revelation:

> *The adversaries of the Lord shall be broken to pieces; out of heaven shall he*

*thunder upon them: the Lord shall judge
the ends of the earth; and he shall give
strength unto his king, and exalt the horn of
his anointed.*

1 Samuel 2:10

The word for anointed is "Messiah," and never
before had Israel known that they had a Messiah.
The first person to receive a revelation that God was
going to send a Messiah is mentioned twice in this
chapter. (vv. 10,35.)

When you loan anything to the Lord, He pays
high interest rates. Proverbs 19:17 says, *He that
hath pity upon the poor lendeth unto the Lord; and
that which he hath given will he pay him again.*
Hannah loaned her son to the Lord forever. God said,
"You don't loan Me anything that I'm not going to
give back to you." This revelation of the Messiah
was the first installment on that loan.

After Hannah left Samuel at the temple with Eli,
she went back home. Samuel lived with Eli, Hophni,
and Phinehas. We would have said that was a
terrible environment in which to leave a little child.
It was an awful atmosphere! Hophni and Phinehas
were committing adultery with the women coming in
to worship at the temple! They were stealing from
the people. They were drunk most of the time, and all
of them were fatter than a forty-pound robin because
everyone in the family was a glutton.

There was young Samuel living in that atmosphere. He was a young, impressionable child. But what had Hannah planted for Samuel? She had planted seed that said he would serve the Lord all the days of his life. She planted that seed, and it had to come up! She was going to get results because the Word is greater than any environment or circumstances. Even if Samuel inherited some bad traits from Elkanah, the Word is greater than heredity. If you have planted the Word and will stand uncompromisingly on it, **it will come up!**

Samuel was in the worst possible atmosphere, but look at what he was doing:

> But Samuel ministered before the Lord, being a child, girded with a linen ephod.

> Moreover, his mother made him a little coat, and brought it to him from year to year, when she came up with her husband to offer the yearly sacrifice (vv. 18,19).

Every year Hannah came up and brought Samuel a little coat because he would have outgrown last year's. History tells us that Ramah was noted for weaving seamless coats. Every year Hannah wove a seamless coat for her son, and when you study Samuel's life you will see that he was always known by his mantle. I think that as he grew older, his mother didn't stop making coats for him. She made them whenever they were needed by her son.

Hannah got some more interest from the Lord because the Bible says that Eli blessed her and her husband:

> And Eli blessed Elkanah and his wife, and said, The Lord give thee seed of this woman for the loan which is lent to the Lord. And they went unto their own home.

> And the Lord visited Hannah, so that she conceived, and bare three sons and two daughters. And the child Samuel grew before the Lord (vv. 20,21).

Look at that interest rate! She bore six children all together, and she had only asked for one! When she loaned the first one to the Lord, she received five more in return. And the last comment made here about Samuel says that he "grew before the Lord."

The Bible says something else about Samuel, which was also said about Jesus:

> And the child Samuel grew on, and was in favour both with the Lord, and also with men (v. 26).

Isn't that what the Bible said about Jesus? (Luke 2:52.) That's why I like to pray that scripture for my children. Hannah had planted that seed for Samuel, and it had to come up. Plant that seed for your children, and it will come up for you too. If you don't sow, you won't reap.

Once a prophet came to Eli and said, "Eli, God is very unhappy with you. You have not corrected your sons." Eli had not sown the Word in his sons, so there was nothing to come up. Good results won't come automatically. You have to take the Word and sow it before it will come up. **You** have to do it. It can't be done for you by someone else. Eli didn't sow any Word in his children, and they turned out bad.

The prophet said, "God is displeased with you, Eli, and He is going to cut off Hophni and Phinehas in one day. They will both die the same day because in this life they have lived in evil together. Eli, you have honored your children more than you have honored God." (1 Sam. 2:34.)

When you honor your children and want what they want more than what the Word says they can have, you are going to be in trouble. God warned Eli that something terrible was going to happen because of the sinful things his sons were doing.

Samuel's Ministry

Samuel was very active in his ministry. His ministry was not something very showy. He had many menial tasks to do, plus waiting on Eli, Hophni, and Phinehas. One night while he was sleeping (he lived in the temple with Eli), a voice called to him, "Samuel." (1 Sam. 3:1-18.) He got out of bed and ran to Eli and asked him, "Did you call me?"

"No, I didn't. Go back to bed."

This happened two more times. Finally Samuel was sure that Eli must have called him:

"Eli, you did call me," he said.

"No, Samuel, I didn't call you, but maybe the Lord is speaking to you. If you hear that voice again say, 'Speak Lord; for thy servant heareth.' "

When God spoke to Samuel the fourth time, what He told him really wasn't good news. He said, "Samuel, something terrible is going to happen to this household because Eli won't repent. I sent someone to talk to him, but he wouldn't repent. His boys are worse. I am going to have to cut them off in one day, and the house of Eli shall not continue as priests."

Samuel was so bothered by that word, he couldn't sleep. He stayed up all night. The next morning he opened the doors of the temple, and Eli came to him and said, "Samuel, did the Lord speak to you last night?"

"Yes, He did."

"Samuel, tell me what He said, and don't spare me."

Samuel told him the terrible news, and Eli said, "God's will be done."

Now the word of the Lord became very real in Samuel's life. As a young man, he grew in the Word.

That isn't surprising because his mother planted good seed before he was even born. The time to plant seed for your children is before they are conceived. The time to plant the Word for your grandchildren is before your children are even married! The Bible says that God's Word will not depart out of our mouth, nor out of our seed's mouth, nor out of the mouth of our seed's seed. (Is. 59:21.) I've been quoting that scripture for my grandchildren, and my daughter Sarah is only 13!

Now is the time to plant seed. If you wait until your children are teenagers to plant seed, they may grow up and become involved in things you don't want. You may find yourself praying, "Oh, God, don't let them do it!" Pray it **now**, and you won't face that dilemma later!

The Philistines came down to attack Israel, and the Bible says that it was just terrible. There were so many of them! And Eli, Hophni, and Phinehas got together to fight them. Of course, Eli was so old that he had to stay home, but the two boys went out and led the battle.

The Israelites were frightened about fighting the Philistines, so Hophni and Phinehas thought, *What can we do to rally the people?* Someone said, "Run home and get the Ark of the Covenant."

When the Ark arrived, the people shouted, but they should have repented instead! They went out to fight, and they lost. Among those who were killed were Hophni and Phinehas, just as was prophesied. It would have been averted if Eli had repented.

Eli was sitting on a stool at the gate of the city, waiting for news of the battle. A man came running in, and Eli asked him how the battle had gone. The man said, "I hate to tell you, Eli, but Hophni and Phinehas have been killed, and the Ark has been taken by the Philistines."

When Eli heard that news, he fell off the stool backwards and broke his neck. When the news reached Eli's daughter-in-law, the wife of Phinehas, who was pregnant and close to the time of delivery, she went into premature labor and died in childbirth. As she lay dying, she said to her attendants, "Call the child Ichabod, for the glory of God has departed because we have lost the Ark." (1 Sam. 4:1-22.)

The glory of God hadn't departed! The ministers had failed, but even if ministers fail, the ministry will go on.

Sometimes people say to me, "Have you heard about Brother So-and-So? He left his wife and isn't in the ministry anymore! That really disappoints me. I feel like giving up."

Well, who is your confidence in anyway? That minister? Or the Lord? My confidence is in the Word of God — not in men.

People are so eager to attack a Christian who has been wounded. I've begun to think about that. In the whole history of the world the only people I have ever heard of who devour their wounded are the Christians. Everyone else tries to help their wounded, but Christians just chew on those that have been wounded by the Devil. They bite on them and gossip about them. That's terrible! God didn't tell us to eat the wounded Christians. He told us to help them and to pray for them.

Phinehas' wife died saying, "The glory of God has departed." But I would have said, "No! You're wrong. There's still Samuel! He has the Word of God planted in his heart, and this isn't the end. This is the beginning of something better!" And all because a mother planted some good seed for her child.

Samuel took over then. He was a marvelous prophet. He lived at Ramah, and the Bible doesn't say whether his parents were still living. In fact, Hannah is never mentioned again. Samuel traveled from Dan in the north, down to Beer-sheba in the south, and he ministered to the people. He prayed for them, and he moved in such miraculous power that when the Israelites had a fight with the Philistines, they called Samuel to go out and pray. When he prayed, it thundered and the enemy got so scared they ran off. The Israelites didn't have to be bothered with the Philistines because Samuel was such a man of faith that he just prayed and that took care of things. They even got the Ark back! (1 Sam. 7:1-17.)

As Samuel grew older, he had two sons who weren't very good. That's terrible to say, but the Bible is honest. The people were discontented, and they said, "Samuel, we'd like to have a king, and your sons aren't that good. You're old and are going to die. We want a king just like the other nations have." (1 Sam. 8:4,5.)

Samuel was human — he felt hurt and rejected. When he went before the Lord about this matter, the Lord told him, "Samuel, the people haven't rejected you. They have rejected Me. I'm their real king. But I'll give them the king they want." Then the Lord encouraged Samuel. (vv. 7,8.)

Samuel was old now. He couldn't do much, and he had taken his sons out of the priesthood because of their actions. The people had forgotten him and all the work he had done all those years. But remember that his mother had dedicated him to be in the ministry **forever**. Now it seems that he is not in the ministry. But wait, He isn't out yet! He started a Bible school at Ramah, and every major prophet in the Old Testament came out of that school! Isaiah, Ezekiel, Elijah, Elisha — all of them came from Samuel's Bible school.

Did you ever wonder how David knew how to read and write and sing songs and play a harp? He learned at Samuel's Bible school. Samuel didn't retire at all — he re-**fired!** He had the greatest ministry at the end of his life because through his school he produced every major prophet that you read about in the Old Testament!

Samuel died, but God kept talking about him! One time God spoke about three people who were outstanding intercessors: "Moses and Aaron and Samuel prayed, and I would listen to them." (Ps. 99:6.) God named Samuel among the great men of prayer.

Samuel never retired, and he isn't retired today. We're still reading the Scriptures written by people he helped to educate. Every time you read the Book of Isaiah and get excited, remember that Samuel started it, and it all goes back to Hannah who said, "God, if You will give me a son, I'll loan him to You all the days of his life."

The Christian's Secret of a Happy Home

At the very beginning of this study of Hannah and Samuel, I mentioned that the meaning of Ramah was "the mount of the watchers." Samuel was called a "seer" because he was born on the "mount of the watchers." He saw things from God that no one else saw.

God will take your circumstances and make them work for you. He will take your environment and make it for you, not against you. He will take your heredity and make it work for you, **if** you will take His Word and make it the number one part of your life. **The Word will not fail!**

I want to share something very personal with you. At one time I began to pray a certain scripture for our son Mike. It was one that I had never noticed before, but I found it while searching the Word for a scripture to pray during a time of difficulty with him.

The verse is found in the Book of Psalms:

> The Lord is righteous: he hath cut asunder the cords of the wicked.
> *Psalm 129:4*

I began to pray and confess that God had cut asunder the cords of lying and other bad things that I knew Mike was doing. Every day I thanked God that those things were cut asunder and that Mike was set free from them. I didn't know all of the things he was involved in, but I knew that God did. And I knew that the Word works regardless of the circumstances.

Mike was eighteen at the time. He was adopted. We had gotten him when he was three and a half years old. He was a diabetic, which was one of the reasons we got him. It seems that no one wanted a diabetic child. They told us that he would die by age twelve, but we didn't take their word for that. We prayed together and he was totally healed. He has never been bothered with it since, and the doctors have verified that he is cured of it.

But Mike was a problem to us. If you said, "Mike, do this," he could find ten ways to do just the opposite, and smile all the time he was doing it. He was sweet, but he rebelled all the way and was very difficult to handle. When he hit his teen years, he was even more difficult. So I thought, *This is ridiculous. I'm just going to start praying the Word and cut those cords asunder.*

One night about two months later, Mike came home after being out with some friends from our church. He called my husband downstairs. It was late in the evening. He said, "Dad, I have to tell you something. I've been involved in something that you need to know about." He told Wally what he had been doing, and it was really a shock.

My husband called me downstairs and Mike told me about it too. Then he said, "Mother, I know you're thinking that you'll make me stop, but I like to do it, and there's nothing you can do about it."

Wally said very calmly, "Well, we won't make you stop, but you can't live here and do it. You are eighteen, so let me give you some choices to think about. Tomorrow afternoon we'll discuss what you want to do. You could quit school and get a job and go on doing what you're doing. You could get a room someplace, if you think you're ready for that. Or, you could contact your natural father and maybe he would let you keep doing this thing and support you — but we won't."

In my mind I thought, *Oh, Wally, that's so cruel to say to him. You don't even know who his natural father is.* We only knew his name and his age. Mike wouldn't even remember his natural father. That seemed unfair to me for Wally to give him those choices.

After we had prayed with Mike, we went back upstairs. I said, "Wally, you shouldn't have said that about Mike's natural father. You don't even know if his natural father is still living. He would be sixty-five years old now. Plus, we don't know if he even lives in Denver, and we've never seen him."

It was a very upsetting time. Wally picked up the telephone directory, flipped it open, and said, "There he is! That's the one!"

"This is a city of a million people," I said. "There are lots of people with that name. You don't know if that's the one or not."

During the night I was bitten by a bug called "female curiosity." I thought, *Lord, what if that **is** the one? Would it help to talk to him?* I got up early the next morning and sneaked out the telephone directory and went downstairs to call. I didn't want my husband to know what I was doing.

A man answered the phone, and I said, "Is this Mr. So-and-So?"

"Yes, it is."

"I'm not going to tell you my name, but I would like to ask you some questions that you may not want to answer. If you don't, I will understand. You can say, 'Lady, I don't want to talk to you,' and hang up. If you ask me any questions, I'm not going to give you any answers. Would you talk with me?"

I know he must have thought, *What a ding-a-ling.*

"Well," he said, "what do you want to know?"

I said, "Did you have a son named Mike?"

"Yes, I did."

"Did you give him up for adoption?"

"Yes, I did. Is he all right? Is he alive?"

"Yes, he's alive."

He asked, "Are you the mother? Are you the foster mother?"

I answered, "I can't answer any of your questions."

"Please, if you think it would be all right, tell him I love him. I didn't give him up because I didn't love him."

It was really heartbreaking to hear this man. He was very defensive.

"I gave him up because I had to. I don't ever want him to think that I don't love him."

"Well," I said, "I don't know if I can tell him that or not. I don't know if it would be good for me to tell him that."

He said, "If you think it would help for me to see him, I would."

Then I shared the problem we were having with Mike.

"Please," he repeated, "get through to him some way that I love him."

"I don't know," I said. "I might call you back."

I didn't know what to say because I hadn't asked my husband. I was afraid I was going to be in trouble! I hung up, and I was so moved by that man because he had told me, "I had open-heart surgery this year, and I was supposed to die. But I never felt that I would die until I got to see Mike again."

I told my husband what I had done, and he was so tenderhearted. He said, "Marilyn, don't you know it was hard on that man? Let's go talk to Mike."

We went downstairs and I said, "Mike, we just talked to your father." He turned to Wally and said, "What do you mean, Mom? There he is" (pointing to Wally).

"I mean your natural father."

Mike was dumbfounded. "How did you know where he was?"

I said, "We didn't." Then I explained to him what had happened the night before. "Would you like to see him, Mike?"

"I'm afraid," Mike said, "but I want to."

That was on a Friday, and we couldn't do anything over the weekend. On Monday I called his father again. "Could you handle seeing Mike this week?"

"I can see him today at three o'clock."

When Mike came in from school, I said, "Your father would like to see you today."

He said, "Mother, I don't want to go with just you. I want Sarah and Dad to go too. I want us to go as a family." (Even the dog went!)

Mike's father lived in an apartment building near the capitol area in Denver. It was a new building with balconies. When we drove up, there was just one man standing out on the balcony watching. I would never have recognized him; he didn't look like Mike at all. But there was no mistaking who he was. He had the look of a father watching for a son. If you are a parent, you know the look. And I saw that man with those eyes that looked like liquid love.

He said, "Mike, you can ask me any question and I'll answer you. But first you have to know that I love you. You have to know why I gave you up." And he told Mike the whole story. Then he said, "Any questions you want to ask me, I'll answer." I wondered what Mike would ask first and was surprised to hear him ask, "Do I have any brothers or sisters?"

"Yes, you have four half brothers and sisters."

Then Mike's dad turned to my husband and said, "Aren't you a pastor? I knew it was a pastor who adopted Mike. Would you care if I come to your church?"

"We'd be delighted!"

We set up a time, and he came one Sunday morning. Mike waited outside for him. I saved a seat for him up front, and he wanted to sit between Mike and me.

My husband asked him, "Would you care if I introduced you to our congregation?"

"No, I wouldn't mind."

My husband said, "You know this church has been so wonderful to us. You've always prayed for Marilyn and me and Sarah and Mike. But now we have a new member of our family. We adopted Mike, but we've also adopted his father."

Wally introduced Mike's dad. He was adopted by more than one that morning because when Wally invited people to be saved, Mike's dad raised his hand. He prayed the sinner's prayer, and Mike heard him. Mike bought him a Bible, and God is working in his life!

Now, what happened to Mike? He came to me and said, "Oh, Mom, I really know that you and Dad love me."

I always wanted to know what is behind this kind of statement, so I asked, "What do you mean?"

"Well, you wouldn't have looked for my natural father if you didn't love me."

That convinced Mike that we really loved him. Of all the things that we have done for him, that's what convinced him, and that was something we just "stumbled into." Mike has a much more secure feeling now.

One day I said to him, "Honey, you don't look much like your natural father."

"Well," he said, "he's really not my father. *That's* my father [indicating my husband]. Mother, there is one thing I know about Dad [Wally]. I know that he loves me."

All of that came from praying Psalm 129:4. I believe that when I started planting the Word, it started working. I know that I haven't seen the end of its working yet.

Pray the Word. Plant the Word. Once you plant it, I can tell you what will happen. Everything around you will fall into place, and you'll say, "Wow! All I did was pray the Word."

But remember, the Bible says that afflictions, persecutions, the cares of this world, and the deceitfulness of riches will try to pull the seed of the Word out of you. But if you won't let that happen, the seed will come up and produce a hundredfold!

I believe that this is the greatest age anyone has ever lived in because the Word was planted for this age long ago. People are more turned on to the Word today that ever before in history. It is marvelous to see how people are getting into the Word and chewing the meat of the Scriptures. Christians just can't get enough of the Word!

Proverbs 4:18 says, *But the path of the just is as the shining light, that shineth more and more unto the perfect day.*

We're receiving light from God's Word to turn circumstances around in our families. Our homes are shining bright with prayer and the Word. Your home will shine brighter and brighter as you take the Word each day and pray and confess it over each member of your family. **God will give you a harmonious home!**

Word Power
For Your Family

Confess the following Scripture verses
out loud for your family.

God's Covenant For Your Family

God has set before me life and death, blessing and cursing; therefore, I choose life that both my seed and I may live. (Deut. 30:19.)

God goes before me in the spirit and power of Elias; He turns the hearts of the fathers to the children, the disobedient to the wisdom of the just, and makes ready a people prepared for the Lord. (Luke 1:17.)

There shall no evil befall me, neither shall any plague come nigh my dwelling. (Ps. 91:10.)

Houses and riches are the inheritance of fathers; and my prudent wife is from the Lord. (Prov. 19:14.)

I chasten my son while there is hope, and I let not my soul spare for his crying. (Prov. 19:18.)

Wealth and riches shall be in my house, and my righteousness endures forever. (Ps. 112:3.)

Through wisdom is my house built and by understanding it is established. By knowledge the chambers are filled with all precious and pleasant riches. The wicked does not lay in wait against my dwelling, nor spoil my resting place. (Prov. 24:3,4,15.)

The Lord will pass through to smite my enemy; and when He sees the blood on the lintel and on the two side posts, He will pass over the door and will not suffer the destroyer to come into my house to smite me. (Ex. 12:23.)

The wicked are overthrown and are not; but my house shall stand. (Prov. 12:7.)

In my house — the house of the righteous — is much treasure; but in the revenues of the wicked is trouble. (Prov. 15:6.)

There is treasure to be desired and oil in my dwelling. (Prov. 21:20.)

Sex — For Married People Only

I live joyfully all the days of my life with the wife (husband) whom I love, which He has given me under the sun, all the days of my vanity: for that is my portion in this life, and in my labor which I take under the sun. (Eccl. 9:9.)

What therefore God has joined together, no man can put asunder. (Mark 10:9.)

I drink waters out of my own cistern and running waters out of my own well. My fountain is blessed, and I rejoice with the wife of my youth. She is as the loving hind and pleasant roe. Her breasts satisfy me at all times, and I am ravished always with her love. (Prov. 5:15,18,19.)

I render unto my wife (husband) due benevolence, and likewise also my wife (husband) unto me. My wife does not have power of her own body, but I; and likewise also I have not power of my own body, but my wife. We defraud not one another, except it be with consent for a time, that we may give ourselves to fasting and prayer; then come together again that Satan tempt us not for our incontinency. (1 Cor. 7:3-5.)

My desire shall be to my husband. (Gen. 3:16.)

Marriage is honorable in all, and my bed undefiled; but whoremongers and adulterers God will judge. (Heb. 13:4.)

Warming The Nest

The Lord hides not His face from me in the day when I am in trouble. He inclines His ear unto me. In the day when I call, He answers me speedily. (Ps. 102:2.)

I will command my children and my household after me, and they shall keep the way of the Lord, to do justice and judgment; that the Lord may bring upon me that which He has spoken of me. (Gen. 18:19.)

I will guide the house and give no occasion to the adversary to speak reproachfully. (1 Tim. 5:14.)

I have wisdom because those that seek it early shall find it. (Prov. 8:17.)

The mercy of the Lord is from everlasting to everlasting upon me, and His righteousness is unto my children's children. (Ps. 103:17.)

I shall teach God's Word to my children, speaking of it when I sit in my house, when I walk by the way, when I lie down, and when I rise up. I tell my children of it, my children tell their children, and their children another generation. (Deut. 11:19; Joel 1:3.)

I train up my child in the way he should go; and when he is old, he will not depart from it. (Prov. 22:6.)

Whom shall He teach knowledge? and whom shall He make to understand doctrine? Those that are weaned from the milk and drawn from the breasts. (Is. 28:9.)

Foolishness is bound in the heart of a child; but the rod of correction shall drive it far from him. Therefore, I will chasten my son while there is hope and let not my soul spare for his crying. (Prov. 22:15; 19:18.)

If I beat my child with the rod, he shall not die, but I will deliver his soul from hell. (Prov. 23:13,14.)

I provoke not my child to wrath, but bring him up in the nurture and admonition of the Lord, lest he be discouraged. (Eph. 6:4; Col. 3:21.)

The rod and reproof give wisdom, but a child left to himself brings his mother to shame. When the wicked are multiplied, transgression increases; but the righteous shall see their fall. I correct my son, and he shall give me rest; yea, he shall give delight unto my soul. (Prov. 29:15-17.)

God has given us one heart and one way that we may fear Him forever, for our good and for the good of our children after us. (Jer. 32:39.)

My child shall not labor in vain, nor bring forth for trouble; for he is the seed of the blessed of the Lord, and his offspring with him. (Is. 65:23.)

Unconditional Love

Charity never fails. But whether there be prophecies, they shall fail; whether there be tongues, they shall cease; whether there be knowledge, it shall vanish away. (1 Cor. 13:8.)

I let love be without dissimulation. I abhor that which is evil, and I cleave to that which is good. (Rom. 12:9.)

I love and work no ill to my neighbor, because love is the fulfilling of the Law. (Rom. 13:10.)

The love of Christ constrains me, because I thus judge that if one died for all, then were all dead. (2 Cor. 5:14.)

I love others because love is of God; and everyone that loves is born of God and knows God; for in Jesus Christ neither circumcision avails anything, nor uncircumcision, but faith which works by love. (1 John 4:7; Gal. 5:6.)

This I pray: that my love abounds yet more and more in knowledge and in all judgment. I know the love of Christ, which passes knowledge, and I am filled with all the fullness of God. (Phil. 1:9; Eph. 3:19.)

I let brotherly love continue. (Heb. 13:1.)

Handling Parenthood

The Lord is righteous; He has cut asunder the cords of the wicked. (Ps. 129:4.)

All my children shall be taught of the Lord, and great shall be the peace of my children. (Is. 54:13.)

Behold, He has graven me upon the palms of His hands; my walls are continually before Him. My children shall make haste; my destroyers and they that made me waste shall go forth of me. (Is. 49:16,17.)

God will give my children one heart and one way that they may fear Him forever, for the good of them and of their children after them. (Jer. 32:39.)

Because I believe on the Lord Jesus Christ, I shall be saved and my house. (Acts 16:31.)

The seed of the righteous shall be delivered. (Prov. 11:21.)

Then Peter said unto them, Repent, and be baptized every one of you in the name of Jesus Christ for the remission of sins, and you shall receive the gift of the Holy Ghost. For the promise is unto me, and to my children, and to all that are afar off, even as many as the Lord our God shall call. (Acts 2:38,39.)

He shall turn the hearts of the fathers to their children, and the hearts of the children to their fathers. (Mal. 4:6.)

It does not seem evil to me to serve the Lord. I choose this day whom I will serve: As for me and my house, we will serve the Lord. (Josh. 24:15.)

I know that my tabernacle shall be in peace; and I shall visit my habitation and shall not sin. I know also that my seed shall be great and my offspring as the grass of the earth. (Job 5:24,25.)

Praying The Word
For Your Family

Praying the Peace of God
in Your Home

Father, in Jesus' name, I come into Your presence now to thank You for all that You are doing in behalf of my family.

As Your child, I stand before You to receive the provisions You have made for us through the shed blood of Jesus Christ. He washed us clean from sin, sickness, and all that Satan would bring. Thank You, Father.

Your Word says that through wisdom this house is built and through understanding it is established. By knowledge the chambers are filled with all precious and pleasant riches. Wealth and riches shall be in this house, and our righteousness endures forever.

I thank You, Father, that no evil shall befall us, neither shall any plague come nigh this dwelling. The wicked are overthrown and are not, but this house shall stand!

This house is blessed with Your life, Your love, Your joy, and Your peace. The peace of God reigns in each of our lives.

With open hearts, we receive Your perfect will for us. Each day we look to You as the Light that shows us the way through every situation and circumstance that arises.

With boldness, I proclaim this day: *For me and my house, we shall serve the Lord!*

Praying the Will of God
For Your Mate

Father, in Jesus' name, I pray now for my husband/ wife. I thank You that _____(name)_____ is filled with the love of God and that he/she walks worthy of You in all things.

This day _____(name)_____ will be blessed in every situation and circumstance that comes his/her way. I pray that _____(name)_____ is strengthened and reinforced in every area of life — spiritually, emotionally, and physically.

Thank You, Father, for guiding _____(name)_____. He/ she walks each day according to Your perfect will for his/her life.

Thank You, Father, that our union is off limits to Satan. We stand against any maneuver that he might be using against us. In the power of Jesus' name, Satan has been placed under our feet!

In Jesus' name, our marriage is a blessed union, joined in the spirit with Your eternal love. The love we share together as husband and wife is a special experience. The bond of unity that makes the two of us one grows stronger and stronger each passing day.

I pray that our marriage may serve as an example to other Christians — and unbelievers, too — of the way God intends for the marriage relationship to be in this life. *What God has joined together, let not man put asunder!*

Prayer For Your Children

Father, in Jesus' name, I come before You now in behalf of my children, _____(names)_____. Your Word says that children are the heritage of the Lord and that the fruit of the womb is His reward. I accept _____(names)_____ as special gifts from You, Father, and thank You for giving them to me.

According to Your Word, as I train up my children in the way they should go, when they are old, they will not depart from it. I accept that promise now by faith. As I teach _____(names)_____ and bring them up in the nurture and admonition of the Lord, I believe they will grow up to be godly men and women.

Because my children are taught of the Lord, great shall be their peace.

I thank You, Father, for Your guidance in disciplining _____(names)_____. As I correct them in love and admonish them according to Your Word, I pray that they will grow in wisdom, in stature, and in favor with You and with man.

I pray that You give Your angels charge over them each day to accompany them and keep them safe from any maneuver of the Devil. Your Word says that the seed of the righteous shall be delivered!

Because I have chosen to serve You, Lord, I can confidently proclaim: *My seed shall be great and mighty upon the earth!*

For Your Information
Free Monthly Magazine

☐ Please send me your free monthly magazine
   OUTPOURING (including daily devotionals,
   timely articles, and ministry updates)!

Tapes and Books

☐ Please send me Marilyn's latest product catalog.

Mr. & Mrs.
Miss
Mrs.   Please print.
Name Mr._____

Address _____

City_____

State_____ Zip _____

Phone (H) (   ) _____

      (W) (   ) _____

Mail to
Marilyn Hickey Ministries
P.O. Box 17340
Denver, CO 80217
(303) 770-0400

BOOKS BY MARILYN HICKEY

A CRY FOR MIRACLES ($5.95)
ACTS ($7.95)
ANGELS ALL AROUND ($7.95)
BEAT TENSION ($.75)
BE HEALED ($8.95)
BIBLE CAN CHANGE YOU, THE ($12.95)
BOLD MEN WIN ($.75)
BREAK THE GENERATION CURSE ($7.95)
BULLDOG FAITH ($.75)
CHANGE YOUR LIFE ($.75)
CHILDREN WHO HIT THE MARK ($.75)
CONQUERING SETBACKS ($.75)
DAILY DEVOTIONAL ($5.95)
DEAR MARILYN ($5.95)
DIVORCE IS NOT THE ANSWER ($4.95)
ESPECIALLY FOR TODAY'S WOMAN ($14.95)
EXPERIENCE LONG LIFE ($.75)
FASTING & PRAYER ($.75)
FREEDOM FROM BONDAGES ($4.95)
GIFT-WRAPPED FRUIT ($2.00)
GOD'S BENEFIT: HEALING ($.75)
GOD'S COVENANT FOR YOUR FAMILY ($5.95)
GOD'S RX FOR A HURTING HEART ($3.50)
GOD'S SEVEN KEYS TO MAKE YOU RICH ($.75)
HOLD ON TO YOUR DREAM ($.75)
HOW TO BE A MATURE CHRISTIAN ($5.95)
HOW TO BECOME MORE THAN A CONQUEROR ($.75)
HOW TO WIN FRIENDS ($.75)
I CAN BE BORN AGAIN AND SPIRIT FILLED ($.75)
I CAN DARE TO BE AN ACHIEVER ($.75)
KEYS TO HEALING REJECTION ($.75)
KNOW YOUR MINISTRY ($3.50)
MAXIMIZE YOUR DAY . . . GOD'S WAY ($7.95)
NAMES OF GOD ($7.95)
#1 KEY TO SUCCESS—MEDITATION, THE ($3.50)
POWER OF FORGIVENESS, THE ($.75)
POWER OF THE BLOOD, THE ($.75)
RECEIVING RESURRECTION POWER ($.75)
RENEW YOUR MIND ($.75)
SATAN-PROOF YOUR HOME ($7.95)
"SAVE THE FAMILY" PROMISE BOOK ($14.95)
SIGNS IN THE HEAVENS ($5.95)
SOLVING LIFE'S PROBLEMS ($.75)
SPEAK THE WORD ($.75)
STANDING IN THE GAP ($.75)
STORY OF ESTHER, THE ($.75)
WINNING OVER WEIGHT ($.75)
WOMEN OF THE WORD ($.75)
YOUR MIRACLE SOURCE ($3.50)
YOUR PERSONALITY WORKOUT ($5.95)